Preventing Child Abuse

creating a safe place

BETH A. SWAGMAN

FAITH
ALIVE®
Christian Resources

Grand Rapids, Michigan

Acknowledgments:

This revised edition is dedicated to Dr. Bernard and Verna Alberta; Faye Martin; Atie Ott; and Ronald Knol. These friends walked in front of me to show the way; walked in back to keep me from slipping; and walked alongside to help carry the burden. Thank you.

The author gratefully acknowledges the contributions of Mr. Ronald L. Foster, Attorney at Law. His diligent efforts to improve this publication stem from his concern for the safety of children served by nonprofit organizations. Any remaining errors or misstatements of the law are the responsibility of the author.

Disclaimer: The materials in this book sometimes touch legal issues. Laws and the contexts that give rise to them vary across states and provinces. Therefore, the suggested policies in this book may not be consistent with the laws and legal practices in all communities within the United States and Canada. The information and policies contained in this book should not be construed as legal advice or as a substitute for legal advice. Organizations should consult legal counsel before approving and implementing a child safety policy.

Composite Stories: This book contains many anecdotal stories and examples shared with the author over several years and from many sources. The stories and examples are useful to illustrate various issues and to create awareness. However, the stories and examples were altered to protect any individual's identity and, in some cases, an organization's identity.

Preventing Child Abuse: Creating a Safe Place. ©1995, 1997, 2003, 2009, Faith Alive Christian Resources, 2850 Kalamazoo Ave. SE, Grand Rapids, MI 49560. All rights reserved. Printed in the United States of America.

We welcome your comments. Call us at 1-800-333-8300 or e-mail us at editors@ faithaliveresources.org.

Library of Congress Cataloging-in-Publication Data
Swagman, Beth, 1955-
Preventing child abuse : creating a safe place / Beth Swagman. -- Rev. ed.
    p. cm.
ISBN 978-1-59255-417-1
1. Child abuse--Religious aspects--Christianity. 2. Church work with children. I. Title.
BV639.C4S93 2009
261.8'3271--dc22
                                    2009000397

10 9 8 7 6 5

Contents

Preface

The Gospel's Message of Hope

I like the good news Mark gives us in his gospel. His story of Jesus doesn't begin with Christ's birth and early life—not that those events are unimportant or insignificant; Mark just can't wait to tell us about Jesus' ministry and message. With just an introductory comment or two he jumps right into the one thing he's most excited about, the thing Jesus proclaims in his first sermon: "The time has come. The kingdom of God has come near. Repent and believe the good news!"

Into the midst of the kingdoms of this world characterized by selfish use of power, materialistic greed, inordinate luxury on one hand and painful poverty on the other, Jesus brings a new kingdom. Into a world in which the weak were (and are!) often used and abused, where injustice flourished, Jesus offered an alternative way of life; one lived under the loving rule of God and in constant fellowship with God. It's a new kingdom of love and peace, joy and justice, harmony and wholeness.

Jesus proclaimed the presence of this new era, God's kingdom, in Mark 1:14-15. From there Mark goes on to relate in rapid succession one event after another displaying the reality of the kingdom that had come in Jesus Christ. Mark shows us Jesus confronting evil, casting out demons, forgiving sin, healing broken bodies, challenging economic perspectives, raising the dead, stilling storms, ministering with compassion, and, in the midst of all of this adult-oriented activity, *caring for children.*

Yes, caring for children! This too is essential in Christ's new kingdom! "[Jesus] took a little child whom he placed among them. Taking the child in his arms, he said to them, 'Whoever welcomes one of these little children in my name welcomes me; and whoever welcomes me does not welcome me but the one who sent me'" (Mark 9:36-37). In the next chapter, verse 14, Mark again quotes Jesus: "Let the little children come to me, and do not hinder them, for the kingdom of God belongs to such as these."

Even though his kingdom has come, Jesus anticipates those who will refuse to live kingdom lives, especially in their relationship with Christ's "little ones." Some of Christ's sternest words of warning, therefore, have to do with those who mistreat or abuse children. "If anyone causes one of these little ones—those who believe in me—to stumble, it would be better for them if a large millstone were hung around their neck and they were thrown into the sea" (Mark 9:42). It takes no stretch of interpretive imagination to believe that Jesus had in mind "sinning against a child" as well as "causing a child to sin." Child abuse is sinning against a child in a most abhorrent manner. It's a violation of the weakest and most vulnerable of persons through a manipulative use of power and control for selfish purposes. So unacceptable is it in Christ's kingdom that it elicited some of the severest words Jesus ever spoke.

If only sins against children were confined to an unbelieving society! Sadly, however, statistics and stories reveal its real presence within the church—with devastating results to children and to the reputation of the church. A 1992 survey by the Christian Reformed Church indicated that the frequency of child abuse within the church is equal to its occurrence in the general population. The report called upon the church "to publicly acknowledge that the sin of abuse exists among us, [and] to support efforts that such abuse be addressed promptly so that abused and abusers may experience the healing power of God's grace"; it also urged the denomination "to take positive steps to make their congregations safe for all persons" (*Acts of Synod* 1992, p. 673).

The book you have in your hand is one step in that direction. First issued as a three-hole-punched handout in 1995, this new and updated fourth edition suggests that the process for protecting children and youth is constantly undergoing change and improvement. One thing that does remain constant, however, is that the church is called to examine itself and to lead society in addressing both the needs of the abused and the abuser. Much more must be done in these and other areas of this enormous challenge. This book will help.

Read it, share it, implement it—with the earnest prayer, "Thy Kingdom come."

Rev. Edward J. Tamminga

Introduction

We hope this book will provide you with the basis for developing a comprehensive child safety policy. Although this is the fourth edition of *Preventing Child Abuse*, it's just the first time we've widened our audience to include churches *and* nonprofit organizations. As you read further, keep in mind that the policies and procedures we suggest pertain only to churches or nonprofit organizations that sponsor programs for children and youth.

Permit me to digress a moment with a bit of history. In 1992 the Christian Reformed Church in North America (CRCNA) conducted a survey on abuse, the results of which clearly indicated that children are vulnerable to abuse within the context of the church. In 1994, with the creation of the office of Abuse Prevention for the CRCNA, efforts began to establish guidelines for reducing the risk of abuse in congregations. In 1995 the office of Abuse Prevention made available to churches a three-hole-punched handout entitled *The Abuse Prevention Program*, which was expanded and published in 1997 as the first edition of the book you're reading, *Preventing Child Abuse: A Guide for Churches* (now retitled *Preventing Child Abuse: Creating a Safe Place*). Over the years since 1997 the book has been updated and revised—and continues to provide congregations with a comprehensive program for identifying and responding to child abuse in the church.

As a result of this book, hundreds of Christian Reformed churches have developed child safety policies. In addition, countless congregations from other denominations have written policies based on the concepts and policies presented here. The book has also been helpful to many nonprofit organizations that provide care and supervision through programs to children and teenagers, among them 4-H clubs, domestic violence shelters, community theaters, after-school tutoring programs, community-based teen clubs, and teen health clinics.

It's a daunting task to write a child safety policy! Because there are several aspects to abuse prevention, developing a careful policy involves many hours of discussion, planning, and writing. Crafting a purpose statement and setting up program policies—including screening of workers, outlining reporting obligations, and developing clear procedures for working with victims and offenders following a disclosure—all requires careful thought and wording. Child Safety Committees are challenged to write helpful policies that attempt to ensure the safety and protection of children without creating an alarmist environment in which a veteran staff member or volunteer is afraid to hug a child.

Congregations and nonprofit organizations often hesitate to develop and implement a child safety policy. In addition to the lengthy process it requires, here are some typical reasons why many institutions fail to institute policies of their own:

- A congregation or nonprofit organization may be unaware of incidents of abuse within the organization (and, in fact, there may be none to date), which makes developing a policy seem unnecessary.

- A group may often have an unspoken fear that if abuse is openly discussed and abuse policies developed, a child will be more likely to conjure up a story of abuse to retaliate against someone in the organization.

- A congregation or organization may avoid establishing a policy either because it does not understand the liability it could face if abuse happens or because it is concerned that adopting child safety policies will *increase* the church's legal liability.

It's important for churches and nonprofit organizations to heighten their awareness and inform themselves of the realities of child abuse and related legal issues. Keep in mind that the baseline policies in this book are by no means exhaustive, foolproof, or even the most effective in *every* situation. We urge you, whether you're part of a congregation or a nonprofit organization, to modify the policies to fit your unique community and situation.

Although we've offered comprehensive policies and procedures, we cannot guarantee that implementing each policy and procedure will prevent the occurrence of abuse in your particular church or organization. Rather, we have tried to provide you with basic, widely recognized, and accepted policies. We encourage your group to use these policies as a basis for establishing a unique child safe policy that reflects your organization and its commitment to children and youth.

This question inevitably arises, "Are we better off with or without a policy?" You may have asked it yourself! Once a congregation or organization understands the risk of child abuse and the importance of reducing that risk within its own walls and programs, it can hardly turn its back on writing a policy. Know that if you choose *not* to write a policy and a harmful situation does arise, you will face some tough questions as to why no basic steps were taken to prevent that harm to children. On the other hand, if your organization does write a policy, and a harmful situation still arises, you will be able to demonstrate that your organization did earnestly attempt to reduce the risk of harm to children.

Here's a related issue that's just as important as whether or not to have a policy: Is your policy *enforceable* as written? Volunteers, staff, parents, and children and youth should be able to rely on a written policy that will be fully implemented. If people cannot rely on a policy as written, the church or organization's liability may increase rather than decrease.

We've found no hard data to confirm the incidence of child abuse within the facilities of churches and nonprofit organizations. In the 1992 CRCNA survey, conducted by the Calvin College Social Research Center, we learned that 4 percent of sexual abuse victims reported abuse by a church-related abuser. However, the designation of "church-related" was not specific enough to claim that the abuser was, in every case, a volunteer or staff person in that organization. Survey respondents did give some anecdotal examples of sexual abuse by clergy, other church leaders, and church volunteers.

Unfortunately, implementing a child safety policy as a church or organization will not eradicate abuse in the wider community since abuse occurs far more frequently in the home than anywhere else. However, if implementing child safety policies in every church and organization reduces the incidence of child abuse by just 4 percent, that's an important achievement for the protection of our children.

Rationale for Developing a Child Safety Policy

You're reading this introduction, which probably means you're thinking about how to proceed in a way that's helpful for your church or organization. Here are additional reasons for beginning work on a policy:

- *To assist in responding to an incident of abuse*. When an allegation of abuse arises, volunteers and staff need a reliable policy to follow that protects the victim from further harm and offers due process to the accused. Without a policy, it may be difficult to know exactly what to do and who to call when caught up in the intense emotions that follow the disclosure of abuse.

- *To satisfy insurance companies' requirement of a policy.* Following the removal or conviction of a volunteer or staff member accused of child abuse, victims often sue churches and nonprofit organizations, claiming negligence or failure to protect them from harm. Insurance companies now require written policies in order to reduce the risk of abuse and, subsequently, to reduce the risk of liability.

- *To satisfy legal counsel's request for a policy.* Not every civil suit stemming from an allegation of abuse results in a mega-award for the victim. Attorneys who represent churches and organizations with comprehensive child safety policies may plead before a jury that child safety *was* important, policies *were* put into place to reduce the risk, and volunteers and staff *did* comply with the policies. And, despite taking reasonable steps, an incident of abuse still occurred. Incidents like these are unspeakably tragic but not always foreseeable or avoidable—even with a comprehensive policy. Faced with a civil lawsuit, it will be more difficult for legal counsel to defend a church or organization that, for whatever reason, does not have a policy in place.

- *To protect children.* Churches and organizations have a moral imperative to provide reasonable protection for children and youth under their care and supervision. Children may become victims of abuse because of their age, size, lack of strength, lack of emotional and cognitive maturity, race, gender, or lack of personal power or authority. They simply cannot defend themselves against older, stronger teens and adults who have authority and power over them—they need the protective shield that a policy provides.

- *To protect volunteers and staff.* An allegation of abuse harms the reputation of a volunteer or staff person regardless of the outcome of the investigation. If volunteers and staff carefully follow a comprehensive child safety policy, they'll be protected in situations when allegations of abuse arise. For example, a policy that requires two volunteers or staff members to be present in a classroom may protect either one from an allegation because one person is able to corroborate the actions of the other. Each time a church or organization adopts a specific policy or procedure, it says to its volunteers and staff, "You are valued for the work you do, and we do not want you to put yourself in jeopardy."

- *To create an opportunity to talk about abuse and its impact.* We know from relationships with family, friends, and coworkers that it is difficult to solve a problem if people won't talk about it. So, too, child abuse thrives in secrecy. When an offender bribes or threatens a child not to tell the "secret," the offender rationalizes continuing the harm because no one knows and no one can put a stop to it. When a church or organization implements a child safety policy, it gives people an opportunity to learn about child abuse in their community. By talking about the issue and becoming educated about proper responses, a community sends a signal to offenders that they are being watched. Children and youth will feel increasingly confident that they can talk to someone who is there to help.

- *To create a safe haven in the church and organization.* A church or organization that sponsors programs for children and youth does not want to be known as a place where children might be hurt. Organizations that serve children and youth are highly motivated to offer quality programs and opportunities for youth to mature spiritually, to grow in relationship with others, to learn moral values, to build character, and to develop life skills. No one will achieve these goals if the learning environment creates fear and distrust, or if it proves to be unsafe. A reasonable effort to create a safe haven whereby youth mature, learn, and grow includes developing a child safety policy!

This all sounds well and good, right? So let's get started. Here's how this new edition works—it's a bit different from previous editions: In Chapter 1 we lay a foundation for the work of a Child Safety Committee. In Chapter 2 we describe the potential legal and liability issues that can arise in cases of alleged child abuse within an organization. Then, in Chapter 3, we list the various elements that comprise a comprehensive child safety policy; and in Chapter 4, we offer a complete outline, along with suggested policy guidelines, to assist you in developing your own baseline policy. Chapter 5 offers a comprehensive look at the screening process and the protocols that are necessary for volunteers and staff to understand. Chapters 6 and 7 present similar looks at protocols for reporting abuse and responding to reports of abuse in a careful and effective way.

Also new to this edition are appendices that highlight the challenges of dealing with bullying, sexual harassment, and the possibility of abuse in programs for people with disabilities, like Friendship Ministries (see Appendices A through E). You'll want to check out our updated resource suggestions, training materials, and useful forms (Appendices F through AA), many of which are also new to this edition.

One final note—beginning now, we will refer to churches and nonprofit organizations collectively as *organizations*, highlighting any material that refers exclusively to one or the other.

1 Getting Started

Receiving a Mandate

Ready for step one? The first thing you'll need to do is obtain the authority to write a child safety policy. Many projects come to a skidding halt when a draft document ends up in the hands of the organization's governing body—when it was not expecting one. Worse yet, the governing body might think someone did an end-run around them by producing, without permission, a document that has potential legal entanglements. Including the right elements in your policy is important, but first you need permission to gather those elements and formulate a policy. So you'll want to begin by asking the organization's governing body to craft a mandate for a committee appointed to write a child safety policy.

Authority from the organization is important for three reasons. First, the organization's governing body is ultimately accountable for the contents of the policy. Second, liability that arises from the policy often rests with the governing body. Third, the governing body's role is to approve all policies that directly affect the organization's personnel and programs.

Before the governing body issues a mandate, it should be aware of the risks of child abuse occurring in the facility, within the programs, or by the volunteers and staff. Your job of educating begins with the governing body. Once this group understands the issues, their support of the policy and its implementation will help immensely in the establishment of a safe and open environment where abuse is not tolerated.

Forming a Child Safety Committee

Once the governing body of your organization develops a mandate, it needs to appoint a committee of six to eight people whose task it will be to develop a child safety policy. Composition of the committee might include program staff and volunteers, parents with children in the programs, and governing board members. Just as the governing body

- Receiving a Mandate
- Forming a Child Safety Committee
- Beginning the Work

Sample mandate: The governing body announces the appointment of a Child Safety Committee with the mandate to develop policies and procedures that will reduce the risk of child abuse occurring in the facility, in the programs serving youth, or by volunteers and staff associated with the programs.

should be informed in the area of child abuse issues, so should the Child Safety Committee (CSC).

Creating awareness of abuse among the governing body and newly appointed committee members does take time. But don't skip this step. If you do, valuable time may be lost later in the process when discussions bog down because people do not clearly understand the risks of abuse that are inherent in organizations that sponsor programs for children and youth. In addition, the governing body and committee members may feel ill-equipped to defend the policy if they do not understand the dynamics of child abuse that lie behind its existence.

Beginning the Work

As it begins its work, your CSC should consider these key questions:

- What policies will create a safe environment for children and youth who participate in our organization's programs?

- How can our organization modify its facility to create a safe environment for children and youth?

- What policies will protect our volunteers and staff from allegations of abuse?

- What policies will reduce this organization's liability?

Here are some tips for a process that might be helpful as you organize and get started:

Initial meeting:

During your first meeting you'll want to appoint

- a chairperson to organize the meetings and keeps members on task.

- a recorder to take minutes and draft (or combine drafts of) each of the separate policy sections into one document. This is an important task because a document written in one voice is usually clearer and more succinct than one that utilizes several voices.

- a collector to gather documents and information that the CSC will use as it develops and writes a policy. These documents and information might include policies from other organizations, newspaper and magazine articles focused on abuse, the organization's insurance policy, state or provincial child protection laws, pertinent denominational documents, guidelines from an organization's headquarters or national office, and so on.

To avoid burnout, consider scheduling meetings once a month and limiting each meeting to ninety minutes. It can also be helpful to make decisions by consensus, which means it's critical that everyone on the committee understands *what* is being recommended and *why*.

Second meeting:
The second time you meet, focus on your facility (see Appendix F, Facility Walking Tour Checklist).

You'll want to report obvious hazards immediately. The committee should also alert the governing body to the potential need for facility changes or improvements. (The governing body should anticipate some expenditure of funds to coincide with the conclusion of the committee's work and recommendations.)

Taking a facility tour will help committee members identify situations of potential risk to children's safety. It will also help the group identify all of the programs and places where volunteers and staff interface with youth, for example, nursery rooms, classrooms, library, vans or buses, gymnasium, bathrooms, conference room, counseling office, and more. In addition, the facility tour might lead to the identification of structure or facility changes that could reduce the risk of abuse occurring on the premises (see Appendix G, Facility Changes for the Protection of Youth).

Third meeting:
The agenda for your third meeting should include time for committee members to generate a list of the program, facility, and personnel issues that your completed policy needs to cover. Individual members might want to choose the issues for which they would like to draft sections of the policy. Or members may prefer to work in pairs to draft small, specific sections of the document. At subsequent meetings, you'll want to review the sections as a full committee as you pull together the parts that will form the larger policy document.

Progress reports to governing body:
The chairperson of your group should meet with the governing body for regular progress reports. The governing body needs to know the issues the committee struggles with and how the committee is working toward resolution of each issue.

Communication:
In any organization, communication is essential to successful planning and to the implementation of change. This is particularly true when the change required is focused on the prevention of child abuse. One way to communicate your work to others is to gather church members or stakeholders of the organization for dialogue, providing them with

an opportunity to learn about child abuse and abuse prevention and ask questions of your committee. Communication of this sort will be especially important when you have drafted the initial policy statement for your organization. You'll want feedback!

Another good communication device—consider developing a newsletter that informs and educates people about the risks of child abuse and about changes that may be necessary for your organization.

Policy reviews:
Another duty of the CSC is to obtain reviews of the proposed policy by the organization's insurance carrier, the organization's legal counsel or an attorney familiar with child safety issues, and at least one outside source. The insurance company will be concerned with issues that relate to the facility, to transportation, and to the selection of volunteers and staff. Legal counsel will be concerned with reporting procedures as well as with the selection, supervision, and retention of volunteers and staff. An outside person will be an independent and objective reviewer; he or she can give you feedback on flaws, inconsistencies, or omissions in the policy, which will also strengthen the completed document.

Implementing the policy:
While the CSC's main responsibility is to develop the policy, the governing body will likely establish another committee to implement the policy. In some cases, the two committees might overlap in membership. The benefit in establishing two separate committees, however, is that the involvement of more people means greater buy-in for the new policy.

When the governing body approves the policy, it should indicate the date at which the policy goes into effect. It's best if the start date also coincides with the beginning date for implementing screening policies and other general policies.

If liability arises from the policy, civil authorities usually turn to the governing body that is currently administering the policy. Therefore, after the governing body initially approves the policy, subsequent governing bodies should review the document periodically and adapt it as new issues of risk or liability arise.

Training staff and volunteers:
To enhance the success of the policy, the implementation committee should establish a process for educating and training volunteers, staff, parents, other concerned stakeholders, and children and youth before the policy takes effect.

Monitoring and revising the policy:
If the governing body determines a specific portion of the policy is not effective or enforceable, the governing body should revise the statement to make it more effective and enforceable—or the governing body should promptly remove that specific statement. In cases in which something is removed from the policy, the organization should notify its personnel, the parents of participating children and youth, as well as the children and youth, if appropriate. The governing body can be liable for a specific policy statement that remains in the document even though it may be ineffective or unenforceable.

A word of advice and encouragement:
Expect the policy-writing process to take fifteen to eighteen months (no one wants to read this!). Depending on the size of the facility, the number of programs offered, and the number of volunteers and staff, a comprehensive policy may take several months to design and implement. You'll also want the governing body of your organization to carefully examine the finished document before approving it because of the liability that is attached to a child safety policy. Substantial change to an organization's way of doing business *always* takes considerable time and careful communication. Don't cut corners by rushing the design, approval, and implementation of your child safety policy!

A word of caution:
No single policy works well everywhere! The child safety policy that works well in one church or nonprofit organization will not necessarily work well in another church or organization. Sample policies may help your CSC visualize what the final product could look like, but an organization that adopts another organization's document without first examining how well it fits its own setting will often find that it should have "tried it on before buying it." The time you might save by copying another organization's policy that doesn't fit your own organization may actually set your process back by several weeks or months.

Speaking of *copying*, it's unethical and illegal to copy a document or portions of a document and present it as if it's your own work. Furthermore, if a CSC copies a document or a portion of it and it contains material that is adverse to the community's laws or practices, the governing body will be held accountable for approving the material without review and without permission.

2 Child Safety Policies and Liability Issues

It often startles people to speak of liability in the same breath as *child safety policy*.

The thought of liability is enough to turn an organization away from writing a policy. On the other hand, here is the simple truth: an organization that offers child and youth programs has a duty to act with *ordinary and reasonable* care toward the children and youth in those programs. The phrase *ordinary and reasonable care* means doing or not doing what a reasonable person would do or not do in similar circumstances. An individual or organization that fails to provide ordinary and reasonable care may have acted negligently and then may be liable for that negligence.

In this chapter, we'll discuss several liability issues, which are important to know as you undertake writing a policy. So let's begin by exploring more about negligence and liability.

In a case of child abuse, the allegation may lead to a *criminal charge*, a *civil complaint*, or *both*, depending on the particular law allegedly violated and the circumstances. For example, criminal charges could be brought if someone intentionally harms a child, causing obvious bruises or lacerations. A parent could bring a civil complaint for negligence against the organization that hired the alleged abuser if it knew the person had a history of violent behavior. A reasonable person with a duty to provide ordinary and reasonable care would not hire a person with a history of violent behavior to care for children.

A criminal charge is more severe than a civil complaint—and carries with it both a greater burden of proof and a greater penalty. On the other hand, a person or organization found at fault (negligent) in a civil complaint may be responsible (liable) for the harm to another. The remedy for that harm is *damages*, which means money is owed to the injured party.

- General Policies and Liability
- Supervision Policies and Liability
- Screening Policies and Liability
- Reporting Policies and Liability
- Retention or Response Policies and Liability

When a person physically harms a child under his or her care and violates a child protection law, the violation could be a criminal matter. However, if a staff person or volunteer fails to act in an ordinary and reasonably careful way, and a child is injured, the failure to act reasonably could be a negligence issue. If a staff member or volunteer is found at fault (negligent), he or she would be liable; and if liable, he or she must pay damages to the injured party.

Sometimes the burden to provide ordinary and reasonable care is on the organization (routine maintenance of the building and vehicles), and sometimes the burden is on the staff person or volunteer (unattended infant falls from a diapering table). There are also times when the organization is liable for the activities of its staff and volunteers. This is *vicarious liability*, and we'll look at it later.

When an organization offers child and youth programs and appoints or hires people to care for children and youth in its programs, the organization should take steps to protect the children and youth from harm, and the volunteers, staff, and organization from liability.

To reduce the risk of criminal or negligent behavior, an organization needs to be concerned about the selection, supervision, and retention of its staff and volunteers. To bolster its efforts, the organization should be equally concerned about and involved in developing and enforcing a child safety policy. The following issues might arise when we speak of liability as it relates to a child safety policy.

General Policies and Liability

General policies detail the organization's expectations of the volunteers' and staff members' conduct. These expectations focus particularly on the appropriate boundaries between volunteers and staff and the children and youth under their care. General policies can reduce the risk of abusive behavior by volunteers and staff.

The organization can meet its duty to provide ordinary and reasonable care to the youth and children in its programs if staff and volunteers comply with the reasonable standards for that care established in the child safety policy. Liability can arise if general policies are not enforced—or if people in the organization don't adhere to them on a regular basis. If your general policies seem cumbersome or place unreasonable demands on volunteers and staff, they may fail to adhere to the policies. If this should happen and harm occurs to a child or youth as a result, the organization could be held liable for the negligence. The risk of liability increases if the organization knew that the policy was not

What to do?

According to the child safety policy of Grace Church, two adults must serve in the nursery at all times. During midweek Bible study, however, the adults would rather attend the discussion than serve in nursery, so the twelve-year-old daughter of one of the participants sits in the nursery with five children for an hour. Last week, as the girl changed an infant's diaper, a toddler climbed up on a chair, fell, and broke his arm.

Do you think the church's nursery policy should cover midweek events?

- Was this incident avoidable if the nursery policy had been enforced?
- Would the parents of the toddler who fell have a cause of action against the church?
- How might your response change if the toddler had been spanked by the twelve-year-old, resulting in bruises on the child's thigh?

being enforced or followed. The organization can be held liable because it failed a duty to enforce a policy that, *if enforced*, might have prevented the harm or abuse from happening.

Supervision Policies and Liability

An organization establishes supervision policies so it knows what its staff and volunteers are doing. An organization that has a duty to provide ordinary and reasonable care, but does not know what its staff or volunteers are doing, could be liable for *negligent supervision* if a child or youth is injured by or in the presence of a staff member or volunteer who was caring for that person while participating in an organization's program. *An organization generally cannot be liable for the activities of staff or volunteers apart from the scope of their duties with the organization.*

Vicarious liability may be an unfamiliar legal-sounding term to you—but it is an important one to understand. The term means that an employer (or organization) assumes the liability for its employees in some circumstances. If an employee (staff or volunteer), while acting within the scope of his or her duties, harms another person, the employer (organization) can be liable. The theory of *Vicarious liability* is that when an employer or organization hires or selects people to do a task, the employer or organization assumes the risk that people will do their task without harming another. To reduce the risk of an employee (staff or volunteer) harming another, the employer or organization provides adequate training for the task and supervision. Training *and* supervision are essential.

Vicarious liability presents a dilemma for an organization. On the one hand, an organization can be liable for the conduct of its staff and volunteers. On the other hand, the organization can't possibly know every time a staff or volunteer acts outside of the scope of duties assigned to that person. Similarly, the organization is helpless against a staff or volunteer who intentionally ignores a written policy or violates a law. Sometimes, then, an organization can defend against a claim of liability by showing that the employee acted outside the scope of his or her duties or intentionally harmed a child or youth. An organization should keep this in mind when considering the following guidelines:

- A written policy by the organization outlining the scope of staff members' and volunteers' duties is essential to reduce the risk of abuse *and* to reduce the organization's liability by demonstrating that a staff or volunteer's misconduct was an act outside the scope of his or her duties *and* the expectations of the organization. However, if the organization had knowledge of the person's wrongful activities or if the

---

What to do?

A nonprofit organization recruits and sponsors men and women to be mentors to children from single-parent families. The organization assigns Jason to thirteen-year-old Benji. Because Benji takes care of his nine-year-old sister Judy after school, she tags along. Often Jason takes Benji and Judy to his apartment where he fixes supper for them and helps Benji with his homework. After finishing his homework, Benji plays with Jason's PlayStation while Jason and Judy watch television in his bedroom.

- Who is at risk in this scenario?
- What could the organization do to reduce the risk?
- If Jason touches Judy inappropriately, does Judy's mother have a cause of action against Jason? Against the organization?

organization failed a self-imposed obligation to provide training and supervision of the person, the defense becomes much less effective.

- Organizations should train their staff and volunteers in the expectations and scope of their duties. The training can help reduce the risk of abuse, and it can also reduce the risk of liability for the organization by offering a potential avenue of defense.

- Organizations should supervise staff and volunteers. When staff members and volunteers act within the scope of their duties, the risk of abuse decreases. However, risk of liability increases if an organization does not have knowledge of staff and volunteer activities, with whom they're interacting, and under what circumstances.

We'll revisit *vicarious liability* in the next section on Screening Liability.

Screening Policies and Liability

Under a screening policy, an organization gathers information about the volunteers and staff it approves or hires. Both the sufficiency and the enforcement of the organization's screening policies are at issue here. When the supervision of staff and volunteers becomes particularly difficult or challenging, an organization should implement additional screening measures to increase its knowledge about who is caring for children and youth. An organization must also increase its knowledge when staff or a volunteer's duties permit him or her to be alone with a child or youth.

An organization may be liable for *negligent screening* in the following ways:

- By conducting random or inconsistent screening.

- By approving or hiring a person who has a history of misconduct or criminal activity.

- By failing to follow the approved steps for screening prospective staff and volunteers.

Now, let's revisit *vicarious liability*. Earlier, in the context of supervision, we noted that

What to do?

Read the following scenarios and decide whether to accept or reject this applicant. Explain your decision.

- Penny is a thirty-five-year-old applicant for a position as tutor of junior high students. When Penny was nineteen and in college, she was arrested for drunk and disorderly conduct during an anti-government rally. She served a thirty-day jail sentence.

- Roger is a forty-one-year-old applicant for a coaching position with minors who are developmentally disabled and hope to compete in statewide athletic activities over the summer. During a reference call, Roger's work supervisor reported that he is frequently late for work, consistently violates the company's no-smoking policy, and is "probably" the cause of one or two female employees asking for reassignments because "Roger likes to tease and doesn't know when to stop."

- Claire is a thirty-year-old applicant for a position working the overnight shift at a domestic violence shelter. When Claire was in college, she shoplifted from a local mall; she pled guilty and paid a fine of $100. After college, Claire became a bank teller. Accused of forging customers' signatures in order to embezzle several thousand dollars, she avoided jail time by performing 100 hours of community service. Claire recently became assistant manager at the fast food restaurant where she now works.

- Ernest is a fifty-two-year-old applicant for a position mentoring teenage boys. Ernest admitted in his interview that he spent twelve years in prison for molesting his ex-wife's ten-year-old daughter. He's been out of prison for five years and states, "I've been clean all that time." Ernest has a spiritual director who wrote a reference saying that Ernest deserves a chance to show the community he has changed.

it could be difficult for an organization to know when or how a staff or volunteer might act outside the scope of his or her duties. When that does happen, an organization's defense may be to demonstrate that the person intentionally acted outside his or her duties and that the harm to a child or young person was not reasonably preventable.

Revisit the four scenarios above and assume that each person was hired or approved for the position. Now if a minor made an accusation of inappropriate touching against any of the four staff members or volunteers, would the prior behavior of any of the four applicants described allow the organization a defense of "not reasonably preventable harm"?

The task is not as easy as you think. If you look only at past sexual misconduct as a predictor of future behavior, that might not be sufficient. A person who previously violated the law might be prone to violate other laws not related to the prior violation. Furthermore, a person's conduct, although not in violation of a law, might indicate an inability to relate in an appropriate way to colleagues or to a child or youth.

These examples point out that:

- An organization's best defense is that it has established a comprehensive safety policy and that it *enforces* the policy. The organization should demonstrate it has adequate documentation of its response to any individual who refuses to *follow* the policy.

- An organization might reduce its liability by demonstrating that a staff or volunteer acted outside of the scope of his or her duties, whether intentionally or not. But that defense is not automatic, and the defense is much less effective if the organization had knowledge that the individual previously tried to act or actually acted outside of the scope of his or her duties.

Developing a thorough and comprehensive screening policy is time-consuming, but, in the end, it is the wisest course of action an organization can take. Developing and implementing a good screening process, however thorough, is not enough. Establishing clear general policies, training staff and volunteers, and exercising ongoing supervision all work together to provide an organization with a powerful tool to diminish the risks of abuse and liability.

Reporting Policies and Liability

By law in many cases and by moral obligation in all cases, an organization has a duty to report a suspicion of child abuse. An organization has a

What to do?

An organization operates several programs including a boys club that reaches out to ten- to twelve-year-old boys identified by the police as at risk to join local gangs. The organization hired a former gang member who turned his life around while in prison. In one-on-one meetings with the boys, the ex-gang member boasts about breaking the spirit that makes young boys rebel. Parents are grateful for his aggressive style that seems to produce results. Although his supervisor confronted him once about his techniques, the staff person maintains that these boys only respond to and respect a strong physical presence. The supervisor knows that at least one boy suffered a sprained wrist—supposedly while arm-wrestling. The organization could lose valuable community funding if word gets out that a staff person's conduct might be abusive. If you are the executive director of this organization, what would you do?

- Wait until a parent complains.
- Wait until a boy complains.
- Put a volunteer in with the employee's one-on-one meetings who will report back to you.
- Notify the police.

duty to provide ordinary and reasonable care under the circumstances, and in some communities, it has a legal duty to report. If the organization fails the legal duty or self-imposed moral duty, it may face a claim of negligence and be held liable for breach of the duty and for violation of the law. Liability can arise if an organization claims a duty to report a suspicion of abuse, but then ignores that duty. The organization's liability is compounded if another incident occurs before reporting, after reporting, or if the accused staff or volunteer has a history of misconduct.

A separate legal issue can arise if the organization does not comply with a legal requirement to report, does not cooperate with investigating officials, acts to cover up evidence, or delays disclosure of information that's important to the investigation.

Retention or Response Policies and Liability

Retention or response policies detail how an organization responds after a volunteer or staff person is accused of misconduct or child abuse. An organization has a duty to protect the accuser and other children and youth in the program from future abuse by the accused. One way to offer protection to the child involved is to limit or prohibit the accused person's activities with that child or other children or youth. The organization could remove the accused person temporarily from the program or facility until an investigation determines the facts in the case. If an organization fails a duty to provide ordinary and reasonable care by protecting children or youth from a possible source of harm, it can be negligent and held liable. This negligence is *negligent retention*.

Conclusion

As you move forward to help your organization develop a policy, keep in mind that it is wise to approve reasonable and practical policy statements because staff and volunteers will more likely follow them. Make these your buzz words: be reasonable and practical.

If you feel overwhelmed by the liability issues, one way to feel more confident is to prepare a policy and then obtain a legal review by a lawyer who is knowledgeable in this area. A legal review provides another layer of assurance that your organization has done a thorough job of reducing the risk of abuse in your facility, within your programs, or by the volunteers and staff.

If you find that a policy already in place has not proved useful, do not ignore that policy. Sometimes changes to the policy may be necessary, but often the simple process of educating staff and volunteers about the policy may suffice to elicit compliance. In addition, it's a good idea for an organization to periodically review its child safety policy with an insurance agent and an attorney familiar with the areas of law implicated by the policy. These people may have suggestions to revive or revise your policy.

An organization might like the comfort of basing their policy on court cases. We've found that the body of case law in many of these areas is very small. Civil cases in particular evolve over months and sometimes years. In addition, courts often encourage attorneys to settle civil cases outside of the courtroom, so we don't hear about them. Sometimes an issue of interest or importance to you won't come to a trial. Instead, you should continue contact with your legal counsel to learn whether a court in your jurisdiction reviewed a particular issue that may have implications for your policy.

What to do?
A parent approached an official of an organization with a concern about the interaction between her daughter and a volunteer. The official listened intently and told the parent he would discuss the matter with the volunteer. He did so, and later contacted the parent with the message that apparently the interaction was a misunderstanding between the teen and the volunteer. The official also told the parent he had asked the volunteer to curtail interaction with the girl; however, the girl tells her mother that the volunteer continues to interact with her. Six months later, another parent approaches the same official with similar concerns about the same volunteer. What should the official do now?

3 What Goes Into a Child Safety Policy?

Chapter 2 touched on the five basic areas of policy formation, relating each one to organizational liability—general policies, supervision policies, screening policies, reporting policies, and response policies. In Chapter 3 we'll highlight additional policy elements that will help you design a complete policy aimed at maximizing the effectiveness of the component parts. Taken together the separate elements will form a comprehensive policy designed to reduce both the incidence of abuse and the potential liability of volunteers, staff, and your entire organization.

- Your Philosophy
- Defining Abuse
- Personnel Summary
- General Policies
- Discipline Policy
- Supervision Policy
- Transportation Policy
- Screening Policy
- Reporting Policy
- Response Policy
- Appendices to the Policy

Your Philosophy

Begin by stating your organization's philosophy, its statement of purpose and intent in developing and implementing a child safety policy. If your organization is a congregation, your purpose statement will likely be based on religious, biblical, or doctrinal principles. If you represent a nonprofit organization, your mission statement may stand as the purpose behind the policy you intend to develop. Or, perhaps your organization will base the purpose statement of your policy on a set of values or a belief system that's held as part of a larger, national organization.

Think of your purpose statement as a two-sided coin. On the one hand it needs to describe the beneficiaries of the policy—the children and youth served by the various programs of your organization. That's side one— you wish to protect children and youth from harm because acts of abuse and misconduct can result in devastating and long-term consequences in their lives. On the other side of the coin, your organization will want to protect volunteers and staff from high-risk activities in which allegations of abuse might arise. On this side of the coin, an unsubstantiated claim of abuse can result in long-term consequences too—the reputations of your staff and volunteers, as well as your organization's reputation, are on the line.

Make sure your philosophy statement also includes the organization's perspective on the extent of the policy application. If your policy extends only to events that take place on the organization's property, within its programs, or with its volunteers or staff, that has come to be known as following the *Inside Rule*. If, however, your policy extends to covering reports of harm by children and youth that has happened to them off the property (in their home, at school, by a babysitter, and so on), that is known as following the *Outside Rule*. Organizations that apply the policy to both scenarios follow the *Inside/Outside Rule*.

For example, if a ten-year-old child comes to a volunteer in your organization and reports a sexual assault in the home by a relative, should the volunteer make a report on behalf of the child (Outside Rule)? Or, is the philosophy of your organization to inform the child that he or she should ask someone who's not part of your organization to report the incident (Inside Rule)? Before leaping to the conclusion that the latter seems heartless, it's important to understand that an organization might choose to follow the Inside Rule in order to reduce its liability. If an organization casts a wider net of duty, choosing to report abuse beyond its boundaries, the risk increases that reporting may become frivolous, that a report may be overlooked, or that a report may be incorrectly made—all of these are circumstances which might result in claims of negligence being brought against an individual or the organization. If you do write the Inside/Outside Rule into your policy, the best course of action is to support it with a careful policy statement and quality training for staff and volunteers.

Here's another reminder for your organization, which we'll talk about at greater length below (see Reporting Policy) and again in Chapter 6: If staff and/or volunteers in your (U.S.) organization are *mandated reporters* in your state, they are *required* to report situations of suspected abuse regardless of who the alleged abuser is and where the abuse took place. Similarly, in Canada everyone is legally responsible to report—regardless of the alleged abuser or the location of the abuse. Thus establishing an Inside Rule policy is a moot point.

Defining Abuse

You'll want to be very clear as you define the types of abuse your policy addresses. To write this section well, your organization should check out your state or provincial law on child abuse. Such laws contain non-specific language, giving judges the opportunity to apply the law according to the facts of the case. Therefore your child safety committee should consider drafting a generic description of abuse, with specific examples, that the public can easily understand.

Personnel Summary

In this section of the policy you should detail the volunteer and staff positions in your organization that will be affected by the overall child safety policy.

Generally, there are three categories of personnel to consider:

- The first category consists of individuals who are paid to care for and supervise children or youth attending the organization's programs. These individuals are known as *staff*.

- The second category consists of individuals who are *not* paid, though they too care for and supervise children and youth. This category may be subdivided depending on the age of the individuals doing the work. Adults who are not paid for care and supervision functions are known as *volunteers*. (In most states and provinces, the age of adulthood is eighteen.) Minors who are not paid for care and supervision responsibilities are known as *helpers*. Helpers should be at least fourteen years old and should not provide care or supervision without an adult present or available to oversee their work. It's important to use these terms consistently throughout the policy document. Confusion results when volunteers are referred to later as *leaders*, *supervisors*, *aides*, *teachers*, or *caregivers* in different sections of the document.

- The third personnel category includes the nonprofit or ministry's executive leadership and governing body. Whether or not to include this group is an area of current debate in church and nonprofit organizations. The argument *against* inclusion is that these individuals do not directly care for or supervise children and youth in the organization's programs. (If they do have responsibility in this area, they should also be included in one of the above categories.) The argument *for* inclusion is for purposes of screening. Nonprofit organizations prefer to avoid the potential public relations fiasco that results from the exposure of a board member with a history of misconduct.

Organizations hold executive leadership and board members to a higher standard of ethical and moral conduct. You've probably heard the term *fiduciary*, a duty of these individuals that implies that they are committed to act in the best interests of the whole organization or of the persons they serve. Further, the fiduciary duty ascribed to leadership and board members in ministry organizations is enhanced by biblical teachings. Christians emphasize the power and authority given to the executive leadership and board members as representative agents of Jesus Christ. Thus, if an executive leader or board member, even apart from relating to

The **Inside/Outside Rule** also impacts the definition and types of abuse that an organization writes into its policy. If an organization responds only to allegations against a volunteer or staff person (Inside Rule), which form of abuse would probably not be defined and included in the policy? If you guessed "neglect," you're correct. Neglect occurs when a caregiver fails to provide for the basic daily needs of a child such as food, clothing, shelter, medical care, and so on. Because an organization and its volunteers and staff are not responsible for providing for the basic needs of a child on a daily basis, the organization with only an Inside Rule would likely not include a statement on neglect in its policy. When an organization uses the Inside/Outside Rule, however, it should define neglect as part of its policy because volunteers or staff may become aware of a child neglected at home (Outside Rule), and that may be sufficient grounds for making a report.

children and youth in the organization, discloses a history of misconduct (such as an extramarital affair), abuse, or criminal activity (such as driving while intoxicated), that knowledge will negatively affect the entire organization.

General Policies

In this section of your document, you'll need to list and describe the programs covered by the broad policy and define the specific policies you'll put into effect within each program. The general policies should state the expectations for volunteers and staff serving in each program. The policies should set clear and unambiguous boundaries for healthy interaction between program personnel and the children and youth within the programs.

Discipline Policy

In this section, you'll carefully describe the discipline procedures that volunteers and staff may use with children and youth in the programs. Whenever an organization offers programs for kids, misbehavior will become an issue. Anecdotally, we know that allegations of physical abuse by a volunteer or staff member often arise around an incident in which discipline was exercised.

The conduct of staff, volunteers, and helpers is the proper subject of the child safety policy, but an organization must also be aware that misbehavior on the part of some kids affects other children and youth in the programs as well. (For a closer look at the problem of bullying and its effects, see Appendix A.)

Supervision Policy

In this section you'll need to address the supervision of program staff and volunteers who relate to children and youth as a part of your organizational activities. While the subject of supervision is usually dealt with under general policies (such as requiring two adults in nursery or in a vehicle), some situations can be identified as posing a greater risk to children or youth, either because volunteers and youth will be outside the facility or because a volunteer might be alone with a child for a time. Your policy should identify such higher-risk situations and the steps it will take to supervise staff and volunteers and to ensure protection for children and youth.

Note: While the "two-person rule" is a Best Practices Rule, organizations need to be creative when confronted with situations in which the rule cannot apply. Organizations may use sign-in sheets, cell phones, reporting forms, activity sheets, the buddy system, and other means for making sure that volunteers and staff are held accountable in such circumstances.

Transportation Policy

As part of your policy, your organization will need to indicate how children and youth are to be transported by volunteers and staff to and from program events. A transportation policy addresses several concerns, among them the expected number of volunteers and youth in the vehicle for optimum safety, a process for verifying the driving records of staff, and confirmation of the adequacy of insurance policies on the vehicles. The policy should also state expectations for the use of seatbelts and child safety seats, as well as air bag restrictions for seating children in vehicles. State and provincial regulations can vary quite a bit, so be sure when writing your transportation policy that your policy conforms to your state or province's child and passenger safety regulations.

Screening Policy

In this section your committee will want to list the criteria for approving and hiring volunteers and staff who serve youth. The policy should identify the person/position that will review screening information, conduct interviews and reference checks, and approve the applicants. The policy should also specify how and where all application materials are stored once the hiring process has been completed.

Your organization should clearly state in the policy that it reserves the right to reject any applicant for any reason including prior criminal convictions. Similarly, you should write into the policy that your organization grants an applicant the right to withdraw from the application process without being penalized in the future should the person want to reapply.

When organizations screen applicants, some information obtained is not sensitive because it is common knowledge—addresses, phone numbers, and so forth. Other information, however, can be sensitive; organizations should err on the side of protecting such screening information from general scrutiny. Remember, though, that your organization may encounter difficulty if it *promises* that information obtained in the application process will be confidential.

An organization can encourage protected communication by asking an applicant to sign a waiver to release from liability persons you ask to provide a reference. The waiver of liability encourages the person giving the reference to speak candidly without fear of reprisal. The purpose of the waiver is to assure both the reference giver and the organization

While a volunteer may have fewer legal protections than a paid employee, organizations may not disregard U.S. and Canadian federal civil rights laws that protect certain classes of individuals from discrimination based on race, religion, gender, ethnicity, and so on. If your organization is unclear about its response to these protected individuals, consult an attorney.

that if the applicant is denied the position, he or she will hold harmless both the person who gave the reference and the organization. You'll want to make sure that in situations in which the reference provider gives information alerting the organization to performance or conduct concerns, the information will be disclosed to those who make the hiring decision and those who may eventually supervise the applicant.

Keep in mind that an applicant may feel more protective of sensitive information in dealing with a small, nonprofit organization that functions without a human resources department. Applicants may feel that fewer legal protections exist for them in such settings. You can counter this perception by clearly describing the approval process, how records are stored, who has access to them, and how breaching this privacy may result in discipline.

Increasingly, many applicants are uncomfortable revealing social security numbers, dates of birth, driver's license numbers, and so on because of the fear of identity theft and misuse of private information. Look for more information on this issue in Chapter 5.

How long is a criminal record check effective? It's out of date the moment your organization receives it! From that moment forward, a person could be convicted of a crime—and only a repeat criminal record check will reveal that latest conviction.

Another growing concern is how often to repeat screening procedures. Most screening material does not need updating unless an individual changes positions within the organization. If new information about the volunteer or staff becomes available, add it to the personnel file. And, unless instructed otherwise, repeat the process of criminal record checks every three years. (You may want to consult your insurance carrier who may have a different standard for repeating screening procedures.)

Reporting Policy

This section of your policy should inform volunteers and staff of the organization's expectations for reporting suspected child abuse. It's important to articulate clear guidelines, including the time frame for making a report and the person to whom the report must be made. You can obtain helpful information for this section from your state or provincial laws on child protection. In addition, you'll want to give staff and volunteers a copy of your organization's Incident Report Form, which will help guide them in the event they need to make a report. (See Appendix H for a sample incident report form.)

In the United States, to locate child protection laws, go to *www.virtusonline.org*. Click on reporting child abuse and then click on the appropriate state. In Canada, for a quick reference and general overview of the child protection law, visit the Ministry of Children and Youth Services website at *www.children.gov.on.ca/*. Specifically, in British Columbia, the child protection law is called the Child, Family and Community Service Act. In Alberta, the child protection law is called the Child, Youth, and Family Enhancement Act. In Ontario, the child protection law is called the Child and Family Services Act.

If you're developing a policy for a Canadian group, remember that everyone is *legally responsible* to report suspected abuse. In the United States, however, child protection laws may provide for mandated reporters and non-mandated (permissive) reporters. If state law refers to mandated reporters, those reporters are generally members of professional groups, such as teachers, doctors, nurses, and social workers, who are required by law to report suspected child abuse, regardless of where the alleged abuse took place or who the abuser happened to be. Permissive reporters are *encouraged* to report suspected abuse. Each organization's governing board should familiarize itself with the laws regarding reporting suspected child abuse in their community. (See Chapter 6 for more information about reporting child abuse.)

Response Policy

What happens when a staff member or volunteer in your organization is accused of abuse? It's important that your policy includes the steps you'll take to respond to such allegations. You may need to respond to three different parties: the alleged victim, the alleged offender, and the organization's constituency. Very often both the family of the accuser and that of the accused, as well as the organization's personnel, will also become involved and will need a response from the organization. When the alleged offender is a staff member or volunteer, articulating and following the steps to respond to that person are important also in protecting the accuser, reducing the risk of re-offense to others, and reducing the organization's liability.

It's difficult to delineate a specific policy for addressing alleged victims because circumstances vary. In addition, investigative procedures, the involvement of law enforcement, and the advice of legal counsel all have the potential to curtail the organization's response to the alleged victim and family. Although the organization probably desires to respond to the alleged victim, its response may be limited by a variety of outside factors.

It's also essential to write media guidelines and a disclosure policy into your child safety policy to ensure a clear and positive way to communicate with congregations and communities when allegations or incidents do arise. Check out the following resources for responding to the three groups mentioned above:

- Responding to an alleged victim (see Appendix I).

- Responding to an alleged offender (see Chapter 7 for references to retention, dismissal, and duty to warn).

- Responding to the congregation and/or constituent community (see Chapter 7, sections on media guidelines; see also Appendix J and Appendices K and L).

A helpful exercise. . .
Child safety committees have found it helpful to wrestle with case studies as they work to construct policy statements that serve their organizations. Check out the three case studies in Appendix P and use the discussion questions to help you focus your energy and efforts on issues that are important to your church or organization.

Appendices to the Policy

In the last section of your policy, be sure to provide a list of resources, procedures, and general information that complement the policy and enhance the reader's understanding of its principles and procedures. Here's a list of some items you might want to append to your completed policy:

- Signs and symptoms of abuse (see Appendix M).
- Code of ethics for staff and volunteers (see Appendices N and O).
- Application forms, other screening forms (see Appendices T, U, and V).
- Incident report, medical consent, and transportation consent forms (see Appendices H, Q, and R).
- Local resources and phone numbers for reporting abuse.
- Policy that stipulates the circumstances in which another organization might use the facilities of your organization.

4 Writing Your Own Child Safety Policy

In this chapter we offer the following policies that form the core of a typical child safety policy. Feel free to draw from these statements, using them as a foundation for developing a comprehensive policy that meets the particular circumstances and needs of the child and youth programs that are a part of your organization. As you set to work, you'll probably find this chapter to be most helpful!

Definitions of Abuse

Here are some common definitions of abuse you might wish to use (or edit to fit your organization's purpose and programs):

- *Physical abuse*—a non-accidental human act by a person responsible to care for or supervise a child or youth, which results in physical pain or injury to that child or youth whether or not it leaves a cut or wound, or a mark or a bruise. Physically abusive behavior ranges from slapping, pushing, shoving, punching, kicking, and biting to more severe forms of abuse like choking, severe spanking, beating, hitting with an object, burning, stabbing, and shooting.

- *Physical neglect*—failure to meet the physical needs of a child or youth for whom a person is responsible. Typically, physical needs include adequate food, shelter, and clothing. Long-term neglect can interfere with or prevent a child's normal development; neglect can also occur when children or youth are denied medical or dental care or prevented from attending school.

- *Sexual abuse*—any sexual intimacy forced on a child or youth or the exploitation of children and youth for sexual stimulation or gratification by a person responsible for their care or supervision. Sexual abuse refers to taking advantage of a person who is not capable of understanding sexual acts or of resisting coercion by a person who threatens or offers gifts. Sexual abuse may or may not involve physical contact. Examples of *non-physical* sexual abuse include displaying pornographic material, photographing a child for pornographic purposes, making obscene telephone calls, and requesting someone to

- Definitions of Abuse
- Definitions of Personnel Terms
- Policy Guidelines for Infant and Nursery Programs
- Policy Guidelines for Preschool Programs
- Policy Guidelines for Children's Programs
- Policy Guidelines for Off-Site Programs (for children ages 5-12)
- Policy Guidelines for Early Teen/ Junior High Programs
- Policy Guidelines for Older Teen/ Senior High Programs
- Policy Guidelines for Off-Site Programs (for youth ages 13-18)
- Policy Guidelines for Out-of-Town Activities
- Policy Guidelines for Mentoring or Tutoring Programs
- Policy Guidelines for Using Hall Monitors
- Guidelines for a Discipline Policy
- Guidelines for a Transportation Policy
- Guidelines for a Screening Policy
- Guidelines for a Reporting Policy
- Guidelines for a Responding Policy
- Guidelines for a Duty to Warn Policy

engage in sexual activity where no physical contact occurs. Examples of *physical* sexual abuse include prolonged hugging and kissing a child; fondling of breasts, genitals, buttocks; sexual intercourse; oral and anal sex.

- *Emotional abuse*—attempts on the part of the abuser to control a child or youth through words, threats, and fear, or to destroy a person's self-worth through humiliation, degradation, and deprivation. Emotional abuse weakens a child's mental and physical ability to resist the offender, cuts off his or her contact with others, making it difficult to seek help, and diminishes the self-esteem of the victim—all of which reinforces a sense of helplessness and dependence on the abuser.

Definitions of Personnel Terms

Here are some common definitions of personnel terms you might wish to use (or edit to fit your organization's purpose and programs):

- *Adults*: individuals eighteen years or older (by most state and provincial laws).

- *Minors*: individuals under eighteen years of age (by most state and provincial laws).

- *Volunteers*: adults who serve without compensation in a child or youth program and provide care or supervision of minors.

- *Staff*: adults who are compensated to serve in a child or youth program and provide care or supervision of minors.

- *Helpers*: minors, ages fourteen to seventeen, who serve in a child or youth program without compensation. While helpers may serve in child/youth programs, they do not provide care or supervision without an adult present.

- *Governing body*: individuals granted oversight of the organization by its articles of incorporation, bylaws, election, or appointment. Individuals usually serve a term of office and may be reappointed.

Policy Guidelines for Infant and Nursery Programs

Consider including the following in your written policy:

- Each nursery session should be staffed by at least two people—either two adults or one adult with one helper.

- One adult (staff person or volunteer) should be present for every four infants.

- One adult or helper should be present for every four toddlers.

- Helpers may serve in nursery only when a volunteer or staff member is present to supervise.

- A third, unrelated volunteer or helper should be present when married couples serve in the nursery.

- A volunteer or helper may not spend time in the nursery room(s) when he or she is not scheduled to serve.

- A staff member or volunteer may take children out of the nursery only for a compelling reason, such as to use the bathroom or in case of illness.

- When toddlers require bathroom assistance in a location outside the nursery, a staff member or volunteer may assist the child and should leave the bathroom door ajar. When the bathroom is located in the nursery itself, a staff member, volunteer, or helper may assist the child, again leaving the bathroom door ajar. Staff, volunteers, or helpers should diaper infants or toddlers in the nursery room.

Policy Guidelines for Preschool Programs

Consider including the following in your written policy:

- At least two volunteers/staff or one adult and one helper should be present in the room. The recommended ratio of adults to children is two to ten.

- A third, unrelated volunteer or helper should be present when married couples serve together in one room.

- If a child needs bathroom assistance during the program session, a volunteer or helper may assist the child with the bathroom door ajar. Children should be encouraged to use the bathroom, with the assistance of a parent, before the session begins.

- Volunteers or helpers may take children from the classroom only for a compelling reason, such as to use the bathroom or in case of illness.

- When children's programs are in session, the meeting room doors should allow for unobstructed views of the room.

- The discipline section of the organization's child safety policy applies to programs for preschool children.

Policy Guidelines for Children's Programs

Consider including the following in your written policy:

- At least one volunteer or staff member should supervise the children in the room. A helper may be present; however, he or she should be at least four years older than the oldest child in the room. The recommended ratio is one to ten; some activities may require additional volunteers or helpers.

- Helpers should not meet privately with children in the facility or off-site.

- Volunteers and staff members should not meet privately with children off-site. Nor should they meet frequently or have lengthy private meetings with children on the premises. When a private meeting on the premises is necessary, it should be held with the knowledge and consent of the child's parent(s) and with the knowledge of the staff member or volunteer's supervisor.

- Volunteers and staff should identify and address bullying behavior observed in their programs.

- Displays of affection toward the children should be limited to such actions as a brief hug, an arm around the shoulder, an open-hand pat on the back, a handclasp, a high-five, or a light touch to the forearm. Volunteers, staff, helpers, and children should respect the other person's right to refuse a display of affection.

- When children's programs are in session, meeting room doors should allow for an unobstructed view of the room.

- The discipline section of the organization's child safety policy applies to programs for school-age children.

Policy Guidelines for Off-Site Programs (for children ages 5–12)

Consider including the following in your written policy:

- At least one volunteer or staff person and one helper who is at least four years older than the oldest program participant should supervise the children.

- When meeting off-site, a program must serve a minimum group of three children.

- Volunteers, staff, and helpers should not meet alone off-site with a child.

- A volunteer or staff person will notify the parent if a child's behavior warrants removal from an off-site program; a staff member or volunteer must be present with the child until the parent arrives to pick up the child.

- Children should not leave the program site unless they are accompanied by a parent, a volunteer, or a staff member.

- Programs held off-site should adhere to the same safety guidelines as those held in facilities operated by the organization. Off-site facilities should present documentation of the premise's liability insurance coverage to the organization prior to the program's start.

- Volunteers and staff members who transport children to and from the off-site location should follow the Transportation Policy of the organization. (See Appendix R for sample transportation consent form.)

- The organization should receive written consent from parents of children attending off-site programs. (See Appendix Q for a sample consent form.)

- Children attending off-site programs should use bathroom facilities without assistance. For a child who needs assistance, a parent should develop an assistance plan with a volunteer or staff member.

- The discipline section of the organization's child safety policy applies to off-site programs for school-age children.

Policy Guidelines for Early Teen/Junior High Programs

Consider including the following in your written policy:

- At least two volunteers or staff persons should supervise activities for early teens or junior high youth. The number of adult volunteers or staff should be greater for off-site activities. Volunteers or staff members should always conduct program activities with sufficient supervision.

- Volunteers and staff members should identify and address bullying behavior when it happens among teens in the program.

- Volunteers and staff should not meet alone with teens in a residence; however volunteers or staff may meet alone with teens in the organization's facility under the following circumstances:

    ▶ with the permission of the teen's parent or guardian;

    ▶ with the knowledge of the volunteer or staff person's supervisor; and,

    ▶ when other staff or volunteers are present in the facility at the time.

- Displays of affection on the part of a volunteer or staff person toward a teen should be limited to such actions as a brief hug, an arm around the shoulders, an open-hand pat on the back, a handclasp or handshake, or a light touch to the forearm. A volunteer or staff member should not single out one teen for affection. Affection should not occur in private settings or isolated contexts. A volunteer, staff member, or teen will respect the other person's right to refuse a display of affection. Volunteers and staff should not encourage displays of affection in a group context that may intimidate, manipulate, or frighten a teen.

- Whenever teen programs are in session, there must be an unobstructed view of the room in which they are meeting.

- The discipline section of the organization's child safety policy applies to programs for early teens and junior high youth.

Policy Guidelines for Older Teen/Senior High Programs

Consider including the following in your written policy:

- At least two volunteers or staff persons should supervise older teens or senior high program activities. (The number of adult volunteers or staff should be greater for off-site activities.) Volunteers and staff should conduct program activities only with sufficient supervision.

- Volunteers and staff members should be at least four years older than the oldest program participant.

- Volunteers and staff should identify and address bullying behavior among teens in the program and should also sponsor training about the topic for the teens in the program.

- Volunteers and staff members should point out and define abusive behavior for the teens in the program and should also sponsor training about the topic.

- Volunteers and staff should not meet alone with teens in a residence. Volunteers and staff may meet alone with a teen under the following conditions:

  ▶ with the permission of the youth's parent or guardian;

  ▶ with the knowledge of the volunteer or staff person's supervisor;

  ▶ in a public facility in the presence of others;

  ▶ no more than once per week; and

  ▶ no longer than one hour per meeting.

- Regardless of the relative ages of the teens in the program, it is not appropriate for a volunteer or staff member to date a teen participant or a close friend of a program participant.

- Displays of affection on the part of a volunteer or staff member toward a teen should be limited to such actions as a brief hug, an arm around the shoulders, an open hand pat on the back, a handclasp or handshake, or a light touch to the forearm. A volunteer or staff member should not single out one teen for affection. Affection should not be displayed in private settings or isolated contexts. A volunteer, staff member, or teen will respect the other person's right to refuse such a display of affection. Volunteers and staff should not encourage displays of affection in a group context that may intimidate, manipulate, or frighten a teen.

- Volunteers, staff, and youth should not privately exchange gifts, phone calls, letters, e-mails, text messages, or other communication that is perceived as intimate in nature. Consider all communications with teens as subject to parental and organizational oversight.

- Volunteers and staff who consume alcohol or use illegal drugs in the presence of youth or offer any of the same to youth during program activities or events shall be subject to discipline and may be reported to the civil authorities.

- Teens who consume alcohol or use illegal drugs on the premises of the organization or during scheduled activities will be dismissed from the program and may be reported to the civil authorities.

- Whenever a teen program is in session, there must be an unobstructed view of the room in which the group is meeting.

- The discipline section of the organization's child safety policy applies to programs for teens and senior high youth.

Policy Guidelines for Off-Site Programs (serving youth ages 13–18)

Consider including the following in your written policy:

- Activities held off-site and away from the organization's facility should adhere to the same safety considerations as activities held on-site.

- The number of volunteers and staff members present should be greater for off-site activities.

- Volunteers and staff members should not participate in an off-site activity with just one teen without having a supervision plan approved by the volunteer or staff member's supervisor.

- Parents or guardians of youth participating in off-site events must be notified prior to each event.

Policy Guidelines for Out-of-Town Activities

Your child safety policy should give special attention to events and program activities that take place outside the local community and require travel within or outside the state or province. Children and youth are more vulnerable to harm and susceptible to negative influences when they're in an unfamiliar place and lacking the protection of family members nearby. Consider the following guidelines for such occasions:

- Events or program activities held out of town require the presence of a greater number of volunteers and staff members than events held on site.

- One volunteer or staff person and one child or youth should not be alone together in a vehicle, on a work-site, in an enclosed room, in sleeping quarters, or in any other setting in which their activity is not observable.

- Males and females should always maintain separate sleeping quarters; supervision of female sleeping quarters should be handled only by women; supervision of male sleeping quarters only by men.

- When sharing a tent or cabin:

  ▸ all children or youth participants should be within two years of age of each other.

  ▸ unrelated children or teens should not share a sleeping bag, cot, or bed.

  ▸ volunteers and staff members should not share a tent, sleeping bag, or bed with a child or teen to whom they are not related.

- When possible, children under thirteen should use the buddy system when using bathrooms and shower facilities that are located away from sleeping quarters.

- Two volunteers or staff members should work together to handle counseling and discipline matters with youth.

- Staff and volunteers should document the content of their counseling conversations with youth, as well as their disciplinary interventions. They should return their logs to the organization after the event and review them with a supervisor.

Policy Guidelines for Mentoring or Tutoring Programs

Consider including the following in your policy:
- A staff member or volunteer may mentor or tutor a child or youth when the following apply:

  ▸ the person has education, training, or experience in a related area that will be of help to the child or teen;

- ▶ the person schedules meetings in the organization's facility and arranges to have at least one other adult present in the facility at the time of the meeting;

- ▶ the person meets with the child or youth in a room with the door open or with a view through the door into the room;

- ▶ the person does not meet with the child or youth in a residence or other unsupervised setting; and

- ▶ the person schedules meetings with the knowledge and consent of a supervisor.

- Staff or volunteers must inform parents of the intent to mentor or tutor a child or teen, and parents must given written consent to the mentoring or tutoring activity. The staff person or volunteer will regularly inform the parent(s) of the child or youth's progress

- Staff or volunteers and the children and youth they mentor should not exchange intimate gifts or gifts of value. The organization and the parents of children in the programs should also be responsible to monitor the exchange of gifts between program staff or volunteers and the children and youth with whom they work.

- Staff or volunteers and the children and youth they mentor should limit expressions of affection as if under the scrutiny of parents and the organization.

- Staff or volunteers must inform parents if a child or youth expresses thoughts of harming self or others, including thoughts of abusive conduct toward others.

- Staff or volunteers must inform parents if they suspect the children or youth they mentor of using drugs, alcohol, or pornography

Policy Guidelines for Using Hall Monitors

Consider using the following in your policy:
- Prospective hall monitors should go through the organization's screening process before serving in this role.

- Hall monitors should always wear an identification badge.

- Hall monitors should report to a designated supervisor.

- At least one hall monitor on duty will conduct facility checks whenever a youth program is in session.

- Hall monitor duties are as follows:

▶ To periodically check all meeting rooms until children and youth have left the facility. A check consists of looking into the room through the door or window in the door.

▶ To periodically check bathrooms until all programs end and children/youth leave the facility. A check consists of opening the bathroom door and looking inside. Men will not check women's bathrooms without someone else present; women will not check men's bathrooms without someone else present.

▶ To periodically check unoccupied meeting rooms until the program ends and all the children and youth have left. A check consists of opening the door to the room and turning on the lights.

▶ To escort a child to the bathroom when necessary.

▶ To direct children or youth found in the hallway to their meeting rooms when programs are in session.

▶ To report suspicious activity to the designated supervisor.

Guidelines for a Discipline Policy

Consider including the following in your discipline policy:

• This organization's policy is to permit no corporal punishment (spanking, slapping, hitting, kicking, punching, and so on).

• This organization's policy is to permit no harsh words, insults, belittling comments, threatening words, or other verbal humiliation of children and youth.

• Staff should inform the parent(s) whenever a child or teen misbehaves beyond minor correction or if a pattern of misbehavior becomes apparent.

• Staff members and volunteers should report to a supervisor all concerns about a child or teen's unacceptable behavior as well as the appropriate response taken to deal with the behavior.

• An additional volunteer or a parent should be involved with groups or present for activities in which misbehavior is an ongoing problem.

• Expectations for the behavior of children and youth should reflect their age and level of comprehension. Similarly, discipline measures should be appropriate to the age comprehension abilities of the children and youth involved.

- Staff and volunteers should regularly remind children of the behavior that is acceptable for the setting. Older children and youth may benefit from having these expectations in written form.

- New volunteers and staff members should be trained in the area of discipline and the use of appropriate discipline measures. Existing staff should receive periodic reminders as well.

- Volunteers and staff should try to avoid physical contact or discipline of a child or teen. Some ways to do this include:

  ▶ distracting the child or youth with another activity;

  ▶ helping the child or youth focus on more acceptable behavior;

  ▶ removing the child or youth from others if another volunteer or staff is available to assist.

- When using timeouts with younger children, the time period should not last longer (in minutes) than the age of the child. (For example, a three-year-old should not have to sit for a timeout any longer than three minutes.)

- Staff or volunteers should immediately remove a child or teen who assaults, harasses, or bullies another person. The bullying child or teen may be reinstated in the group when the risk to others has been adequately reduced.

- Staff or volunteers may remove a child or teen from a program at any time for any reason; reinstatement is optional. A child or teen may be reinstated if the risk of re-offense has been adequately reduced.

Guidelines for a Transportation Policy

The transportation policy you develop should apply to all volunteers and staff members who transport children and youth (who are not relatives of the volunteer or staff) to or from sponsored activities. Consider using the following statements in your transportation policy:

- When transporting children and youth:

  ▶ Two volunteers or staff persons will be present and seated in the front seat of the vehicle;

  ▶ At least two youth must be present in the vehicle; or a youth being transported alone must sit in the back seat;

  ▶ A volunteer or staff member will log each pick up and drop off and turn in the completed log to a designated supervisor.

- Volunteers and staff must have a valid driver's license and proof of insurance before transporting children and youth.

See Appendix R for a sample transportation consent form.

One thing to be especially cautious of when transporting children and youth is use of fifteen-passenger vans. The NHTSA and NTSB (national vehicle safety agencies) have issued warnings about the possibility of rollovers in these vans. Nonprofits and churches are often the recipients of older-model fifteen-passenger vans, as schools can no longer use them for safety reason. Organizations must look at these "gifts" very carefully. For more information, go to *http://www.nhtsa.gov/cars/ problems/studies/15PassVans/15Pass Customer.html.*

- The driving records of volunteers and staff members who routinely transport youth will be reviewed annually.

- Volunteers and staff must abide by state and provincial requirements for car seat use, seatbelt use, and air bag safety:

  ▶ Children and youth must wear seatbelts when being transported.

  ▶ Volunteers and staff will not transport in one vehicle more children than there are available seatbelts.

  ▶ Where required by law, car seats must be used for younger children.

  ▶ Children under the age of ten may not sit in the front seat if there is a passenger-side airbag installed in the vehicle.

- Volunteers, staff, adults, and teens who transport relatives to the organization's programs and events are not subject to this policy.

- Parents or guardians who give permission for their child or teen to be transported by a non-related minor with a valid driver's license are not subject to this policy.

Guidelines for a Screening Policy

Consider using the following statements in your policy for screening staff, volunteers, and helpers:

- Written position descriptions will be available for review upon request. When applying for a position, an applicant should meet the qualifications and expectations of the position for which he or she is applying.

- The screening steps applicable to each position will be specified by the organization. Additional screening steps may be put in place if a staff member or volunteer changes positions and/or assumes new responsibilities within the organization.

- An applicant has the right to withdraw from the selection process at any time without prejudice.

- The organization will designate a selection committee whose task is to approve volunteers for available positions. The governing body's task is to hire paid staff persons.

- The organization reserves the right to reject an applicant for any reason. Those reasons include but are not limited to: refusing or failing to complete screening; failing to provide requested information; providing information subsequently determined to be false or misleading; or obtaining information from references or a criminal record check which suggest the applicant is not suitable for the position.

- The organization reserves the right to establish a minimum length of time for membership or residency before an individual applies for a volunteer position.

- The organization reserves the right to reject an applicant for any misdemeanor or felony conviction, for any plea of no contest to a felony or misdemeanor, or while the applicant is under investigation for or charged with a misdemeanor or felony.

- Information obtained through the screening process for volunteer applicants will be stored in a locked file with access limited to those individuals determined by the organization to have access. Personnel files of paid employees will be stored according to any applicable laws and standard business practices.

- The organization will conduct criminal record checks every three years unless otherwise required by liability insurance carrier standards or community practice.

- A volunteer, staff member, governing board member, or member of the selection committee who learns of or has knowledge of prior acts of misconduct by the applicant must report that knowledge to the selection committee.

Guidelines for a Reporting Policy

Depending on the location and circumstances of your program and personnel, choose the appropriate statements to include in your reporting policy:

- In Canada anyone who suspects or has reason to believe that a child has been or is likely to be physically harmed, sexually abused or exploited, or is in need of protection due to specific circumstances, *is legally responsible* to report the matter to a child protection social worker within twenty-four hours.

- In the United States, anyone who suspects or has reason to believe that a child has been harmed or threatened with physical harm, sexual abuse, or exploitation *may* report the matter to Children's Protective Services or to the police within twenty-four hours.

- Some individuals or professions, by state law, are designated as mandated reporters and *must* file a report of suspected child abuse with Children's Protective Services or the police within twenty-four hours.

- A staff member or volunteer with firsthand information regarding suspicion of child abuse is responsible to provide an oral report to civil authorities within twenty-four hours.

- In most circumstances the identity of the person making a report will not be revealed without consent unless required for the purposes of a court hearing. Therefore, the volunteer or staff with firsthand information should phone in the oral report and later fill out and submit the appropriate incident report to Children's Protective Services (CPS) in the United States or Children's Aid Society (CAS) in Canada or to police officials in either country.

- It is the responsibility of the civil investigation team (CPS, CAS, or police) to notify the alleged offender of the allegations made against him or her. Neither the firsthand reporter nor an official of the organization nor the organization's child safety committee should engage the alleged offender in an investigative process until CPS, CAS, or the police first interview him or her. An organization can investigate an allegation of abuse occurring on the organization's premises, in a program offered by the organization, or committed by personnel of the organization.

- After reporting to the CPS, CAS, or police, the volunteer or staff member should either notify an executive of the organization or its child safety committee of the report.

- If a volunteer or staff person is unsure how to respond in a particular case, he or she should contact CPS, CAS, or the police—or speak with a program supervisor or the organization's CSC about the matter. This discussion should take place as soon as possible after hearing information or witnessing behavior leading to a concern or suspicion that child abuse may exist. After discussing the matter with one of the groups suggested earlier, the volunteer or staff person with firsthand information is responsible to report his or her suspicion of child abuse. Furthermore, he or she should not be prohibited from reporting even if the consulting source does not concur.

- State and provincial laws protect a staff person or volunteer from civil suit following a report to a child protection agency or the police. Civil officials, however, can penalize an individual for filing a frivolous or malicious report.

- State and provincial laws authorize civil penalties for failing to report a reasonable suspicion of child abuse. In addition, obstructing or interfering with an investigation of child abuse can result in criminal charges.

In most communities, it's important to notify authorities with an oral report within twenty-four hours of suspicion of child abuse. A written report is required within seventy-two hours.

Guidelines for a Responding Policy

As you develop a policy for responding to volunteers or staff persons against whom allegations have been made, consider using the following statements:

- When a staff person or volunteer admits sexual or physical abuse against a child or youth, the admission of guilt should come to the organization's governing body regardless of whether a formal allegation has been made.

- If a volunteer or staff person confesses to or is found guilty of sexual or physical abuse against a child or youth, that person must be removed from his or her position and barred from further service in that or any similar capacity.

- If the organization's governing body learns from CPS, CAS, or police officials that allegations of abuse merit serious investigation or that there is the possibility of formal charges the governing body should

  ▶ receive written documentation of the allegations and the information known at that point;

  ▶ give the accused an opportunity to confront the allegations; and

  ▶ take one or more of the following steps: prevent contact between the accused and the accuser; supervise the contact between the accused and all other children and youth in the program; temporarily suspend the accused (with pay when applicable) without prejudice pending the outcome of the investigation.

- When the organization's governing body learns from CPS, CAS, or police that criminal charges have been filed against the accused, it's important to take all of the steps included in the organization's policy.

- When the organization's governing body learns from CPS, CAS, or police that criminal proceedings have been concluded,

  ▶ it should decide (in the case of acquittal or dropped charges) whether to rescind or maintain its earlier action.

  ▶ it should terminate (in the case of conviction) the staff person or volunteer's position. The governing body should deny that person future reinstatement or reentry to a position serving children and youth.

- Seek the advice of legal counsel when considering reinstatement, reentry, or re-application by someone who has been previously terminated. (Note that often a terminated volunteer or staff person will seek reinstatement in the church or organization. Be sure to protect your organization by consulting with your legal counsel in such cases, as well as in situations that involve an applicant who has been previously terminated or dismissed by another organization.)

Guidelines for a Duty to Warn Policy

Consider writing the following into your policy:

- The organization may acknowledge to a nonprofit organization that it terminated a volunteer or staff person for substantiated misconduct or abuse against a child or youth.

- The organization shall not deny to a nonprofit organization that it terminated a volunteer or staff person for substantiated misconduct or abuse against a child or youth.

- The organization shall not deny to another nonprofit organization seeking a reference that it terminated the volunteer or staff person in question because of substantiated misconduct or abuse against a child or youth.

5 A Closer Look at Screening

Why develop a screening policy for your organization? There are a number of good reasons. A screening policy serves to inform a concerned congregation or nonprofit constituency that the organization is serious about both preventing abuse and responding to allegations of abuse. In addition, many insurance underwriters and attorneys recommend that the organizations they insure or represent have a written screening policy to reduce liability and potential claims. Parents, too, demand that organizations take careful screening measures to ensure that their children are safe when attending programs. Furthermore, states and provinces encourage (and sometimes require) screening of some professional staff and/or personnel for certain positions. (For example, check out the "National Child Protection Act of 1993" in Appendix S.)

- The Application Process
- The Interview Process
- Reference Checks
- Criminal Record Checks
- Fingerprinting
- Miscellaneous Screening Procedures

For any organization, putting in place a screening policy can have a twofold effect on child abuse prevention. First, selection committees responsible for approving volunteers and new staff for the organization's programs have more data to help them better match a person's interests and skills with an available position. The committee is also in a better position to screen an individual away from a program or a particular position if they believe that person might pose a risk to children.

Second, in some cases, the mere presence of a screening policy is a deterrent to an individual who may pose a threat to children and does not want to risk exposure. Beyond discouraging applicants with a criminal history, screening policies also create other ways for an organization to detect applicants with a history of inappropriate behavior or misconduct.

A screening policy, however, cannot guarantee the prevention of abuse. The goal of a general prevention policy is to reduce the incidence of abuse—and to reduce the liability of volunteers and staff. Organizations should keep both of these goals in mind when developing a screening policy.

The most effective screening process includes five steps: reviewing applications, conducting personal interviews, obtaining reference letters, performing a criminal record check, and fingerprinting, which obtains nationwide information about the applicant's criminal record. An organization should specify in writing the steps of its screening policies and which of these steps apply to each staff, volunteer, and helper position within the organization. (See Appendices X and Y for a chart showing volunteer and staff positions and the recommended screening steps for each.)

Let's take a closer look at each important step.

The Application Process

The basic tool in any screening process is the application form, which requests general information about the applicant and his or her suitability for a position. Applicants for staff or volunteer positions should receive further consideration only after an application form has been completed and submitted. When an organization puts in place a new screening policy, it should require that volunteers already serving in a position will complete an application form. Thereafter, volunteers who continue to serve in the same or similar positions need not repeat the process. (See Appendices T and U for sample volunteer application forms.)

Most information obtained on an application form is neither confidential nor private. Name, address, cell phone number, areas of interest, skills or qualifications, names of references, and so on are examples of information that is public—and that may be expected to be shared.

However, some information you obtain on the application should remain private information shared only with those who need to know. For example, an application form may request applicants to disclose past criminal history or current personal struggles with pornography. This information is necessary for the organization to know as part of the approval process for staff or volunteer positions. It can also be useful to churches offering pastoral care to those who acknowledge personal struggles or past convictions. If a decision is made not to select the applicant in a ministry or church context, and the applicant will likely remain a member or participant in the church's ministry, the church should develop a procedure for handling such denials.

When an organization states on its application form that the information on it is *confidential*, it is implying that the applicant may disclose information without fear that it will be shared. However, a screening

Tip
Organizations may reserve the right to establish a residency or membership requirement for volunteer applicants. For example, a church may require a volunteer be a member of that congregation for at least six months. For a nonprofit organization, residency for at least six months may be a requirement for application.

policy will *never* be effective if the very information that *should* be shared is locked up in a file to protect the applicant.

Who should be required to fill out an application? All adults and minors (fourteen to seventeen years old) who are seeking a volunteer or paid position in a program serving children and youth should fill out an application. The person who will supervise the position should review the application. When possible, a joint review of applications is preferable.

The Interview Process

A personal interview should be required of all applicants for paid positions within the organization. Interviews should also be required of applicants for any volunteer positions with supervisory responsibilities since it's important to assess experience and skills in these areas. Positions designated as *program leaders* or *program directors* certainly require interviews. And, finally, interviews are a must for any applicant whose position will include time alone with children or youth, such as youth counselor, coach, mentor, and so on.

As a rule, interviews should not be discretionary. The organization's screening policy should clearly state when interviews are required—an applicant is entitled to know whether the position he or she is seeking requires an interview. Under certain circumstances, however, a supervisor or executive may make an exception and decide to interview a volunteer applicant for a position that doesn't ordinarily require an interview. For example, an applicant might not list on the application any previous experience working with youth, and the supervisor may choose to explore the applicant's interest in the position by talking with him or her in an interview setting. When a supervisor requests an interview with an applicant who was not expecting one, the supervisor should explain why the interview is necessary.

Further, supervisors cannot pick and choose whom to interview. Skipping interviews with existing volunteers or long-term volunteers because of their familiarity with the organization may later open the door to liability issues for failing to follow established screening procedures.

When possible, the supervisor of the position should conduct the interview. Joint interviews with another supervisor or a volunteer familiar with the position are preferable. At the end of the interview, the supervisor should summarize the applicant's responses in written form and attach them to the application form.

What to do?

Joe and Colleen are foster care parents whose foster daughter reported to the authorities that Joe spied on her while she showered. After several weeks of investigation, the police arrested Joe. However, at Joe's preliminary hearing, the foster daughter refused to cooperate with the authorities, and the magistrate dismissed the charges against Joe.

Should Joe be required to acknowledge his arrest record on a volunteer application form?

Would your response be different if Joe was asked to serve on an agency board, assuming he would not have direct contact with youth?

Note: Although an application form may request an applicant's arrest record, criminal record checks typically reveal only convictions. Someone who has been arrested but later has had the charges dismissed may consider an arrest record prejudicial. We recommend that the application form request information about *convictions*.

Tip
It's standard practice to ask for three references, but how many of them should the supervisor contact? All of them! It's not a waste of time to hear three people describe the positive attributes of an applicant—that might mean the supervisor has the right applicant for a position. What could happen if the supervisor listens to two positive references and decides to stop? If the applicant does not work out and the third reference could have given the supervisor actual knowledge of a pending problem, the organization may view the supervisor's conduct as inviting unnecessary risk.

Reference Checks

For paid positions that require references, applicants should provide the names of three people the organization may contact. Employers, friends, colleagues, and neighbors are good sources for references. Relatives of the applicant, on the other hand, are generally unacceptable references because of their presumed lack of objectivity.

The individual may provide a written reference or an electronic reference letter. Organizations may also obtain a reference by calling the designated person and writing down the information gathered in the phone conversation. The written letters of reference as well as summaries of phone references should be attached to the application form. The application form should include a waiver for the references—or the reference form itself could include a waiver. An applicant should sign the waiver to protect the person providing the reference from any liability and to ensure that the person will provide a candid, truthful assessment of the applicant's suitability.

Should applicants for volunteer positions provide references? The short answer is yes. Applicants for volunteer leadership or supervisory positions should provide references—and so should applicants for positions that involve time alone with children and youth. When a position does not require references, it is permissible to request references under certain circumstances. For example, if during the interview process, the supervisor develops concerns about an applicant's skills or suitability, the supervisor may request references. The supervisor should explain why he or she is requesting references. As in the case of applicant interviews, it's important that the organization write into its policy which positions require references. Supervisors should not randomly choose who will be required to provide references.

Although an applicant knows the names of the people supplied as references, he or she should not be privy to the references' comments. The references' information, however, should be shared with individuals in the organization who need to know. (See Appendix V for a sample reference check form.)

Criminal Record Checks

The fourth step in the screening process, a criminal record check, provides important information. The police will check an applicant's criminal record in the state or province where the applicant resides. A criminal record check reports felony convictions, pleas of no contest, and, often, lesser offenses such as misdemeanors. Some criminal record check forms disclose information reported to Children's Protective

Services or Children's Aid Society. If an applicant has lived in another state or province within the past ten years, it's important to request a criminal record check from there as well. Beyond the ten-year point, consider the age of the applicant at the time and whether a record check from another state or province is necessary.

In recent years, the process for obtaining a criminal record check has changed dramatically. Previously, an applicant would go to the local police agency and fill out a form requesting a criminal record check. The police agency would process the request within a few weeks and return the results to the applicant or to the organization. Today, there are Internet services that conduct criminal record checks for free or for a small fee and present the results within minutes. Some police agencies sponsor an Internet site where criminal record checks can be done. Another option is to use a private company that will conduct exhaustive background checks on the applicant's education, work history, military history, and criminal history. These companies cost more, and some of them require a minimum number of applicants to process before they will offer their services.

Criminal record check forms require an individual to give his or her consent to undergo a criminal record check. The applicant must provide a driver's license number, date of birth, social security number, and any aliases he or she has used. Understandably, applicants for volunteer positions are reluctant to share this sensitive information, especially when it was not required in the past. Organizations find it cheaper and quicker to conduct criminal checks online, but they must cross the hurdle of convincing people to share sensitive information at a time when identity theft is on the rise. If applicants secure their own criminal record check online, they can maintain their privacy; however, self-checks can raise the question of authenticity. Organizations need to consider the merit of receiving information themselves via authentic criminal record checks over against allowing the applicant to control sensitive information by initiating the criminal record check process.

When the completed criminal record check is received, the original should be kept in the applicant's file and a copy of it given to the applicant. The head of human resources, the head of volunteer coordination, and the person with oversight of the position should receive the information prior to the applicant's appointment. A criminal record check that reveals an arrest or conviction must be shared with the staff mentioned above, as well as with the executive director or executive committee of the organization.

Tip

Organizations should be cautious about using a Sex Offender Registry as a *substitute* for a criminal record check. Sex Offender Registries create easy access to a list of the names, addresses, and sometimes pictures of known sexual offenders. The registries, however, contain information only on convictions obtained after the registry law was passed; so many sexual offenders are not listed. These registries are also notorious for inaccuracies because sexual offenders don't always provide the required information or they neglect to update police agencies on their whereabouts.

Here's an example, however, that illustrates the flip side of this discussion. A church leader tried for several months without success to schedule screening for a volunteer in her church. One day, while searching the registry for another applicant, she came across the volunteer's name and recent conviction for a sexual crime.

Another reason to rely on the criminal record check rather than using the Sex Offender Registry alone: the criminal record check reveals whether the person in question has been convicted of other forms of abusive or harmful conduct including child neglect, child physical abuse, assault and battery, domestic violence, drunk driving, weapons violations, and so on. We don't emphasize it enough, but sexual misconduct is not the only form of harm that adults or older teens can cause children.

Tip
A criminal record check is good until the moment it is completed. It does not report any criminal activity that takes place after that time. For that reason, do not accept a criminal record report from an applicant who secured a report more than six months prior to the application.

You should obtain criminal record checks when hiring or approving staff members and volunteers who frequently meet with children and youth. The same is true for the selection of directors of youth programs, pastoral staff and clergy, executive directors, and professional staff. Once an applicant in any of these categories has successfully completed the first three steps of the screening process, be sure to initiate (and complete) a criminal record check before considering an offer of employment or approval for a volunteer position. There are a few exceptions: If your organization employs a bookkeeper, accountant, or treasurer you'll want to do a criminal record check of applicants for those positions. And, if your organization provides transportation for children and youth, you'll want to do checks for persons who will be driving the organization's bus or van.

Organizations should file the authenticated or original criminal record check in the employee's file. If the employee has obtained and submitted the criminal record check, the original goes to the organization and the employee receives a copy. The employee's supervisor should review each criminal record check; and, when concerns arise, the supervisor should seek consultation within the organization as well as from legal counsel, if necessary.

Criminal record checks can be expensive for churches and other nonprofit organizations, although the amount varies from community to community. If an organization (or its insurance carrier) requires all staff and volunteers to obtain a criminal record check, the associated costs can be very high. To add to the burden, organizations should repeat criminal record checks on designated staff and volunteers at least every three years.

As you write a screening policy for your organization, keep in mind that criminal record checks are not sufficient by themselves; screening should include a comprehensive strategy for *really knowing* the people who will supervise and care for the children and youth in your organization. Many people who commit abuses against children are not reported or caught, so the absence of a criminal record does not necessarily mean they've not harmed a child. Similarly, the absence of a criminal record does not guarantee that someone will not harm a child in the future. While it's important that your organization screens applicants in order to reduce the risk of harm, it's also essential that you select staff and volunteers who exhibit the interpersonal and problem-solving skills that will make a contribution to your programs.

Fingerprinting

Fingerprinting, the final step in a comprehensive screening process, may be the most thorough way to identify a known child abuser. Unlike a criminal record check, fingerprinting includes a nationwide check that goes beyond the local state or province. Fingerprinting allows police authorities in states and provinces, the Federal Bureau of Investigation (FBI), the Royal Canadian Mounted Police (RCMP), and state and provincial child protection agencies to offer information about the applicant. Fingerprinting offers organizations the opportunity to find information about an applicant from the widest spectrum of agencies that encounter predators of children.

Some organizations already routinely use fingerprinting to screen applicants. This step has sometimes been instituted after an organization discovers a predator that has been moving from one part of the organization to another—and at each location, reports or allegations of abused children have surfaced. If your organizations is one in which employees or volunteers are prone to "move around" you may want to consider fingerprinting. (In many states and provinces, fingerprinting is mandatory in programs that serve children such as daycare programs, foster care programs, adoption programs, and some nonprofit organizations.)

Fingerprinting is also the most costly and intrusive screening step. So who in your organization should be fingerprinted? Anyone who, by job description or program description, will have frequent or long-term one-to-one contact with children and youth should be fingerprinted. So should any applicant who has lived *at any time during adulthood* in more than two states or provinces.

The request for fingerprinting should come after the first three steps in the screening process have been successfully completed and before an offer of employment or approval of a volunteer is extended. When an organization requests fingerprinting, it eliminates the need for a criminal record check. When your organization receives the results, they should be placed in the applicant's file.

Like the criminal record check results, the fingerprinting results are accurate up to the moment the fingerprinting is completed. However, this process is generally not repeated for staff and volunteers who do not move out of state or province. Instead, your organization should consider conducting a criminal record check at least every three years for the staff and volunteers who remain with the organization.

Tip
See Appendix W for helpful guidelines if you find, as many organizations do, that you need assistance in dealing with the complex issues surrounding the challenge of integrating a known sexual offender into your church or nonprofit organization.

To obtain information about fingerprinting, call the local police authorities in your area.

Miscellaneous Screening Procedures
Creating and Storing Personnel Files

Organizations that use any of the screening steps should keep personnel files on volunteers and staff members. The files should be in a locked file cabinet with limited access granted to those who make employment or approval decisions, those who update the files with new information, and those who access file information for the purpose of conducting an investigation. Individuals who access files without authorization or who disclose information in the files without authorization can create discipline issues for themselves.

In addition, laws also govern an individual's right to access his or her own personnel file. An organization without a human resources department should contact legal counsel when employees wish to review their files.

A personnel file may not be altered or destroyed while the person is employed or volunteering for the organization. After staff members or volunteers leave the organization, their personnel files remain intact in a locked file cabinet. Files may be destroyed after a suitable time period has elapsed. Electronic scanning and storage make it easier to store files of former staff and volunteers without taking up valuable office or file space.

An insurance company or attorney can request or subpoena an individual's personnel file in case of a civil suit or criminal investigation. Caution should be exercised that only verifiable information be placed in a personnel file; if information in a person's file is unsubstantiated, it is best to label it that way. Also take care to identify the time, date, and source of any supporting documentation with regard to an allegation of wrongdoing or inappropriate conduct by an employee or volunteer.

The initial expense of creating personnel files and a storage system is greater than the cost of maintaining the files and system. The start-up may also be labor intensive for support or administrative staff, as are periods in which the organization is heavily involved in recruiting staff and volunteers.

Managing the Selection Process

To avoid confusion (not to mention potential liability) an organization needs to carefully detail its selection process in writing. It's beyond the scope of this book to educate organizations on the hiring process for paid staff, beyond explaining the screening steps described above. We would, however, offer the following additional advice.

Your organization's policy should state the specific steps for screening candidates for each position. It's sufficient and helpful to use a chart or diagram to explain the steps (see Appendices X and Y). The arbitrary omission or addition of screening steps could seriously jeopardize an applicant's perception of the organization's fairness. For example, when screening steps are implemented randomly, volunteer applicants might believe they're being discriminated against.

An applicant for any position, volunteer or otherwise, has the right to withdraw from the application process without prejudice. Similarly, the organization reserves the right to deny an applicant for any reason. However, an organization must exercise this right more carefully with an applicant for a paid position because employment laws are more protective of the rights of prospective paid employees than those of volunteers.

While it may find the task to be cumbersome at first, an organization is wise to develop and make available position descriptions for all staff and volunteer positions. In addition to reducing the risk of abuse, organizations always desire to find suitable matches between positions and applicants. Time constraints can often cause an organization to search rather desperately for anyone to fill a particular position that's open; however, the responsibility of caring for children and for youth definitely includes selecting the best possible candidates who understand children and youth, care about them, and work safely with them.

Finally, one last plug for coordinating and collaborating when putting the screening steps into practice. The combination of information and impressions given by more than one current staff person can result in a wise hiring decision. Steps such as the interview process and obtaining references are best done by more than one person. For example, a male/female team involved in the screening process might detect things that either of them alone might not notice. A supervisor/youth worker team might listen a little differently or have different insights into the person a particular position requires based on their perspective and sensitivities.

6 Understanding the Reporting Process

Your organization should be ever watchful for signs and symptoms of abuse and should *always* respond when children and youth report abuse. When required, the personnel of your organization should refer any suspicion of abuse to someone who has been trained to investigate child abuse complaints, usually the experts with your local police department or child protection agency.

Volunteers or staff in youth programs may find themselves observing an abusive incident, noticing the signs or symptoms of abuse, or receiving a child's or youth's report of abuse. When that happens, volunteers or staff members should *not* conduct their own investigation of the matter—but, again, for their own protection, should follow an established reporting procedure. If your organization assumes responsibility for reporting abuse you should be aware of the potential legal issues and liabilities related to reporting. That's why it's so important to provide staff and volunteers with sufficient training and support for reporting abuse.

Despite showing observable signs of injury, children and youth will often deny that they've been harmed by someone. Some children will not report an abusive incident because they're afraid of the abuser or because they believe they deserved the injury. In addition, abusers will often threaten or bribe a child or youth not to tell anyone about what happened. Many children and youth will not report abuse by a parent or caregiver out of love for or loyalty to that person. Interestingly, young children in particular will not report sexual abuse if the act did not cause pain, because they are more likely to think something is harmful only if it is also painful. If an abuser behaves kindly towards other people or towards that child at other times, the victim may also refrain from reporting an abusive incident, thinking that the abuser had a bad day and didn't intend the harm. Furthermore, children and youth recognize that people who have authority over them can be intimidating, so they're less likely to report abusive behavior in these situations.

- Reporting Suspected Abuse
- The Implications of Reporting
- What to Report
- Guidelines for Calling Authorities
- Consulting the Child Safety Committee

We hope the procedures outlined below will assist the staff and/or volunteers in your church or organization to report quickly and helpfully when encountering situations of suspected child abuse.

Reporting Suspected Abuse

We've included the following definitions to help your staff and volunteers understand their roles and responsibilities regarding reporting.

Mandated Reporters

In the United States, child protection laws state that certain licensed or professional groups, designated as *mandated reporters*, are required to report any reasonable suspicion of abuse. Mandated reporters, when hearing of or witnessing signs or symptoms that raise a suspicion of abuse, *must* report it to police officials or to a child protection agency. Mandated reporters generally include schoolteachers, social workers, day care providers, nurses and physicians, and licensed counselors. (If you're a mandated reporter it's important that you know whether to report only in the context of your professional duties or whether the obligation to report also applies when you're away from your professional duties or functioning as a volunteer at a church or other similar organization.)

In Canada it's different—everyone is legally responsible to report a suspicion of child abuse. Canadian law gives the public the same duty to report as professionals are charged with. However, the law does recognize that professionals may have special awareness of child abuse because of their background or training.

Mandated reporters in the United States and anyone with a legal responsibility to report in Canada can face civil penalties, criminal penalties, or civil liability for failing to report suspected abuse. The keys to answering Molly's "What to do?" question are answers to these questions: First, does Molly have enough information? And second, what may be considered a "reasonable suspicion of abuse"?

"Reasonable suspicion" implies that a reasonable person seeing a similar bruise or hearing a similar story would come to a similar understanding about the probable cause of the bruise or assault. Reasonable suspicion does not imply actual *knowledge* or *certainty*, as in, "I *know* what happened!" Instead, reasonable suspicion suggests that reasonable people have sufficient general knowledge of appropriate and inappropriate interactions to be suspicious about a particular incident.

Don't be too hasty in discounting your conclusions and deciding that your doubt is not "reasonable." In some communities, the use of the

---

What to do?

Molly is an elementary schoolteacher, and she occasionally serves as a church nursery attendant on Sundays. At school Molly is approached by a student who claims that she sleeps with her dad when her mother travels on business. Last week, while serving in the nursery at church, Molly notices bruises on the legs of one of the toddlers.

- Is Molly mandated to report her student's claim?
- Is Molly mandated to report the bruises she observed on the toddler?
- What do you think Molly should do in each situation?

---

term "reasonable" has been dropped because too many people deny their suspicions out of fear of reporting or a wish to protect the alleged abuser. The standard for reporting continues to change because, despite people's best intentions, they are still reluctant to report. That, of course, often leaves children caught in harmful and abusive situations.

Clergy Mandated Reporters

In Canada, clergy are legally responsible to report a suspicion of child abuse. In the United States, some state laws mandate clergy to report while other states do not. Members of the clergy should find out whether they are mandated reporters in the state where they work. Even when states do not mandate clergy to report, however, the child protection law encourages *everyone*, including clergy, to report cases of suspected child abuse. Clergy who are not mandated reporters should consider it their moral and ethical duty to report.

Clergy often make an important distinction when dealing with a person who discloses something to them. If a minor or a third party reveals an incident of abuse, mandated clergy should definitely report. Clergy have refrained from reporting a case of suspected child abuse, however, when the alleged abuser makes a statement acknowledging abusive behavior. Such statements presumably are protected by clergy-penitent privileged communication; thus, the clergy person has not reported the abuse.

When clergy choose to suspend the clergy-penitent privilege in order to report suspected child abuse it's not always clear what the outcome will be. Such occasions are rare, and seldom does the accuser challenge the clergyperson's decision to report. What clouds the issue is whether the denomination represented by the clergyperson adheres to a doctrine or practice of the *confessional*. The courts have typically upheld the right of clergy to hear the confession of an abuser without reporting it when the clergyperson is following a denominational doctrine of the confessional. The courts in particular are not likely to deviate from this position when it is legally based, but tend to leave it to the legislature to amend the statutes that abrogate the right to privileged communication. Presumably, when no such doctrine or practice of the confessional exists, clergy in those denominations may (and should) report suspected child abuse disclosed by the abuser—and with less risk of civil liability.

If a person discloses abusive behavior to clergy in the presence of a third party, the disclosure is not considered privileged and the abuse is reportable. Sometimes an exception may be made if the third party is a spouse; however, spousal immunity for criminal acts, including child abuse, is no longer the shield it once was.

Tip
A legally recognized privileged communication exists for clients or patients of many professionals, including physicians, accountants, attorneys, and mental health specialists. Likewise, a legally recognized clergy-penitent privileged communication extends to parishioners in their conversations with clergy. State laws generally abrogate or do away with the right of privileged communication for most professionals and require them instead to report suspected child abuse. Only a few states also waive the clergy-penitent privilege to permit clergy to report suspected child abuse.

Tip
Clergy and other mandated reporters are required to make an oral report within twenty-four hours of observing signs or hearing a report of suspected child abuse. Mandated reporters should send a written report to officials within forty-eight to seventy-two hours.

Permissive Reporters

In the United States, anyone—even a minor—who is not a mandated reporter *may* report a reasonable suspicion of child abuse. That makes us all *permissive reporters*. Child protection laws indicate that *no one* may be prohibited from reporting a suspicion of child abuse.

Furthermore, a permissive reporter who hears a report or observes signs or symptoms of suspected child abuse should be encouraged to report it to police officials or to a child protection agency immediately. Delaying a report could not only result in additional abuse to the child, it could also diminish the physical evidence of abuse, thus jeopardizing the case. (If bruises or visible injury to the child is present, medical treatment may be necessary. The visible evidence may also help substantiate the allegation of abuse.) As in the case of mandated reporting, an oral report should be made to police officials or a child protection agency within twenty-four hours of observing signs of abuse or receiving a report of abuse. A written report to the same officials or agency should take place within seventy-two hours.

Anyone, including volunteers, staff members, clergypersons, or mandated reporters who receive firsthand information about suspected child abuse, is ordinarily entitled to anonymity at the time of reporting to police officials or to a child protection agency. No one needs to hesitate to fill out the appropriate incident report form and to report to the appropriate officials.

If a non-mandated reporter (including a volunteer or staff member) who has firsthand information asks another person to make the report, the reporter then has anonymity—but anonymity does *not* extend to the person with firsthand information. The person who wants to avoid reporting may find that he or she is subject to additional scrutiny by an investigator who not only wants a report but also an explanation for that person's unwillingness to file it him- or herself. An unfortunate consequence to the child when the firsthand reporter chooses not to report is that the secondhand reporting often delays an investigation until the investigator can track down the person who supplied the firsthand information.

The Implications of Reporting

For individuals

People agonize over whether to report a suspicion of abuse on behalf of a child. It's natural to want to know with greater certainty what *really* happened. It's also normal to be concerned about harming the reputation of a coworker or family member by filing a report. Adults are conscious of the potential chaos and upset that a report of abuse triggers for a family and the entire community—and they don't want the fallout linked with their report. Because they also see other adults, including themselves, as vulnerable to a child's fabricated story of abuse, a decision to protect another person can be seen as a symbolic step toward protecting themselves.

If an adult fears the repercussions of making a report, imagine the terror a child must feel! What will happen to the beloved parent or admired Boy Scout leader? What will happen to *me*? Child abuse victims commonly experience and report a feeling of the rug being pulled out from under them the moment they tell someone of the abuse.

It's true that children sometimes lie in order to retaliate against a parent or other adult. However, such lies rarely take the form of an allegation of abuse. A child or youth will more likely lie to *protect* an adult-abuser or parent-abuser out of love for that person.

Adults lie too. Family members often deny allegations against a spouse or other family member. Family members tend to defend the accused even though they were not witnesses and cannot claim with certainty what actually happened between the alleged abuser and child. Unfortunately, to discredit the claims and prevent investigation, it's also common for family members to blame the child (accuser) for lying or for being selfish or vengeful.

In addition, spouses often defend each other despite deep-seated concerns about the relationship between the partner and one of their children. When a child tells the non-offending parent of abuse, the parent may say, "I'll take care of it"—and then do nothing at all.

Reluctance to acknowledge abuse may extend beyond a family's borders. If a parent depends on an organization's services to the family and to its children in particular, he or she will not be eager to respond to a child's complaint against someone in that organization. Children often report that when they tell their parent about abusive or inappropriate behavior on the part of a staff person or volunteer, the parent warns them not to mention it again. Thankfully, this pattern seems to be lessening as the media reports more stories of abuse; there seems to be a growing awareness that children need our protection.

Often, too, such allegations stun coworkers and fellow volunteers who refuse to believe the charges. Their observations of the accused suggest that the person would never hurt anyone! It's not uncommon

Most false allegations of abuse reported by a child occur in the context of a divorce action or amidst post-divorce difficulties in the broken family.

Tip
A significant danger to the child when informing family members about the child's allegation of abuse is that the family may coerce or threaten the child to either recant the allegation or face "breaking up this family."

for colleagues to speak admiringly of the accused and report the lengths to which that person would go to help a child. Like family, staff and volunteers might also blame the child or teen by using comments like these:

- "Kids lie about this stuff because they don't get their way."

- "That's a troubled kid….what would anyone expect from him?"

- "Girls are so dangerous at that age. They will say or do anything—I don't trust them."

The reality is that offenders lie, too. They have much to lose by admitting they've hurt a child—including their job, their family, their reputation in the community, and their family's image. And the greatest loss could be the offender's personal freedom if he or she is prosecuted and imprisoned. No one has more to gain by lying and thus convincing others not to report their suspicions.

Let's clarify the difference between a *false* report and an *unsubstantiated* report. A false report is a lie—whether by the child or by the reporter who files a report based on information he or she knows is not true. An unsubstantiated report results when a thorough inquiry has been made, but the civil authorities cannot determine whether abuse has actually occurred. There may be some evidence to support the claim of abuse, but not enough to satisfy the standard needed for successful prosecution of criminal charges against the abuser. The incidence of unsubstantiated complaints is far greater than the number of false reports. Successful prosecution is one measure of a substantiated allegation; however, most communities have more unsubstantiated claims than substantiated claims of abuse.

For organizations
Child protection laws generally allow an organization to conduct an investigation following allegations of abuse committed by a volunteer or staff person on the premises or in one of the organization's programs. Organizations, however, do not have the authority to investigate matters that take place in the child or youth's home or between a volunteer or staff person and his or her own child. We caution you not to begin an investigation before you submit a report to police officials or to a child protection agency. It's best to wait to begin an internal investigation until officials have been notified and have begun their own investigation.

Police officials and child protection agencies have the responsibility to contact the alleged offender and present the allegations against him or her. Volunteers, staff (including clergy), organization officials, or

Tip

To prevent reckless harm to reputations and to discourage false reports, child protection laws contain warnings that those who intentionally lie or file frivolous reports risk being prosecuted themselves.

We'd like to stress again that most children do not lie about abuse. Because children are so helpless in abusive situations we should err on the side of helping them—even when we do not know with certainty that the allegation they've reported has happened.

child safety committees should *not* engage the alleged offender in any investigative process until the authorities have interviewed the accused.

Prior to the offender's interview with police or child protection services, your organization should take a hands-off approach. Clergy, board members, staff, or others in your organization who may later be appointed to investigate the allegations should decline to discuss the charges if approached by the accused. Instead, you should encourage the alleged offender to cooperate with officials. It's also wise to advise the alleged offender that any information he or she discloses to you is reportable. If the alleged offender still desires to confess or discuss the allegations, be sure to document your conversation by writing down the person's comments as you meet or immediately afterwards. Confessions of child abuse are reportable to police officials and child protection authorities, even if the official report of suspected abuse was made earlier.

What to Report

Let's explore three basic questions that will help you understand a bit more about how and what to report.

- **First, what should staff members or volunteers report when they observe what appears to be a sign or symptom of abuse?**

When someone in your organization observes signs or symptoms of possible abuse, that person may talk with the child about what he or she has noticed. Although it's appropriate to ask the child how the injury happened, the questioner should not interview the child in detail about it. Instead, he or she should simply note the sign or symptom along with the child's report of how it appeared.

After talking with the child, it's important to write a report that notes signs or symptoms observed, summarizes the conversation with the child, and describes any emotion the child expressed during the conversation. If bruises or injuries are visible, you'll note them, relate the child's report of how the injury occurred, and give your opinion of whether medical treatment seems advisable. Use the written report as reference while talking to the police or a child protection agency. Send the report to the police or child protection agency if they request it; also, give a copy of the report to the person within the organization who is designated to receive it.

- **Second, what should volunteers or staff members report when they hear a story of abuse?**

Tip
If a bruise or injury is not visible or obvious, never ask the child to remove clothing to reveal it.

Tip
No matter what a volunteer or staff observes or a child reports, it's not appropriate to *suggest* to the child that he or she may have been abused.

In order to file a report based on a child's story, a volunteer or staff person should note the answers to the following:

▶ *What* does the child say happened?

▶ *Who* was with the child when it happened?

▶ *Where* did it happen?

▶ *When* did it happen?

Asking children questions in a helpful way is a challenge. Questions that elicit yes or no answers may not be helpful. Nor should you suggest to children the answers to your questions. Frightened children will be sensitive about upsetting adults with their stories. Although children want the adult to believe their reports, they may fear that the adult will become upset and possibly blame them or refuse to believe them. This is one reason why some children tell the story of their abuse without showing much emotion.

On the other hand, trying to tell their stories to adults in a way that calms or pleases the adult often leads children to alter their stories. It's better for children to relay the events in their own words than to be helped by suggestions from the adult that often reflect what the adult *thinks* may have happened. When you talk to children, ask open-ended questions that allow them to recall and talk freely about what happened.

When a child reports a story of alleged abuse, the adult should listen carefully—and write the report later. The report should state the specifics of the child's disclosure, the date of the report, any bruises or injuries observed or reported, and what, if any, affect or emotion the child showed while describing the incident. The reporter should refer to his or her written report while talking to the police or child protection agency. The volunteer or staff person should send the report to the police or child protection agency within forty-eight to seventy-two hours; a copy of the report should also be given to the person designated within the agency to receive it.

- **Third, what should staff members or volunteers report when they observe an incident that may be abusive?**

When someone in your organization observes an incident of abuse within the building or one of the programs, he or she should immediately intervene to assist the child. After the child is cared for, the person who observed the incident should write a report that describes the incident, the intervention, and the conclusion to the incident. The report should also mention any observed bruises or injury to the child. Again, the report should be a reference point for conversation with the police or child protection agency. Send the report to the police or child protection agency and give a copy to the designated person within the organization.

Although it is wise to write down the events as you recall them, remember that notifying the local police or a child protection agency of a reasonable suspicion of abuse must occur within twenty-four hours of an observed or disclosed incident.

You'll want to train volunteers and staff members who may be firsthand reporters that it's important to be prepared to respond to the child, to the family, and to the investigating authorities. (See Appendix I, "Responding to a Child's Report of Abuse," and Appendix Z, "Responding to Families Notified of Alleged Abuse.")

The final step in the reporting process? After reporting to police officials or a child protection agency, the volunteer or staff person should contact a member of your organization's child safety team and inform them of the report.

Tip
If a child is injured during an incident, seeking medical treatment for the child is your *first* priority. Even if the abuser is a family member or relative, contact the police immediately when you realize that the child has been hurt. Quick medical attention is important to help the child, as well as to preserve evidence.

What happens when the authorities choose not to pursue a report? If there is still concern for the child's well-being, the person from your organization who first reported observing signs of abuse or who listened to the child's report of alleged abuse should stay in contact with the child. It is important to keep a written log of any further signs, symptoms, or incidents. Over time, the log may reveal an ongoing pattern of inappropriate behavior, or it may lead to detection of another difficulty in the child's life. Of particular concern will be a pattern of increased frequency or intensity of signs, symptoms, or complaints of abuse. If a reasonable suspicion arises again, report it!

Guidelines for Calling Authorities

Understanding the distinctive roles of the police and the child protection agency is important and helpful. Regardless of the identified abuser, the police and child protection agencies carry on two different, but sometimes overlapping, roles.

The police department actively investigates allegations of abuse and turns over the results of the investigation to the prosecutor or crown prosecutor's office. The prosecutor then decides whether to proceed with charges against the abuser. To charge a person in a criminal matter, the matter must be investigated by the police and reviewed by the prosecutor's office. Then, the matter goes before a judge or magistrate who, upon review of the information submitted, decides to sign either a warrant for arrest or a warrant to obtain additional evidence. Although the standard for proceeding at this point is *probable cause*, it's important to note the number of people and steps that are involved.

The role of child protection agencies, on the other hand, is to ascertain whether the child and any other minors in the home are safe where they are. The agency's investigative role is limited to the *safety* and *wellbeing* of the child(ren) in that home—not the investigation of the alleged abuse. The investigation belongs to the police once the protection agency worker has made a home assessment.

However, a proper determination of safety includes asking the child and other family members about the alleged incident and the events surrounding the complaint. Child protection workers often collect data (and sometimes evidence) that the police and prosecutor find helpful.

If the protection agency worker determines that the child is not safe in the home, he or she must petition the local judge or magistrate for an order to remove the child from the home. The order comes from the court; it's not at the discretion of the protection agency worker to remove a child.

Here are some helpful guidelines for deciding whether to call the police or a child protection agency when reporting suspected child abuse.

- Notify the Children's Protective Services or Children's Aid Society if
   - ▶ the minor is related to the abuser or lives with the abuser.
   - ▶ the minor is being abused by a relative in the minor's home or in the relative's home.
   - ▶ the minor is being abused by a non-relative in a custodial parent's home.
   - ▶ the minor's safety is at risk, and parents are not protecting the minor.
- Notify the local police department if
   - ▶ the minor does not know the abuser.
   - ▶ the minor is not related to the abuser and does not live with the abuser.
   - ▶ the minor may have contact with the non-relative abuser without protection.
   - ▶ the minor is under the authority of the non-relative abuser at a location other than home.

- If the victim reports bruises or injury, it's important to note only those bruises seen without the youth displacing any clothing. Based on observation or the child's report, and if the child needs medical treatment, contact the police regardless of whom the alleged abuser may be.

- If for any reason the report was sent to the wrong agency, be assured that the police or child protection agency will automatically forward the report to the appropriate agency without the need for a duplicate filing or phone call.

Sometimes it's difficult to know if a reasonable suspicion of child abuse does exist in a particular situation. Child protection laws encourage us to report cases of suspected child abuse, and they grant us immunity from civil or criminal liability when we make a report in good faith. Neither police officials nor child protection authorities expect a reporter to know with certainty what has happened to the child. It's the responsibility of the police to investigate and make that determination, if possible; however, to reduce the risk of someone filing a frivolous or malicious complaint that may harm someone's reputation, child protection laws do establish penalties for reports not made in good faith.

Any time a volunteer or staff person is uncertain whether a reasonable suspicion of abuse exists, he or she is encouraged to call police officials or a child protection agency and request to discuss the matter with someone who conducts child abuse investigations. As with many professionals and mandated reporters, volunteers and staff members may find consultation helpful before making a report of suspected child abuse,

Consulting the Child Safety Committee

When a volunteer or staff member is uncertain about making a report, contacting a member of the organization's child safety committee is a good idea. This contact should happen as soon as possible—within twenty-four hours—after the person hears information or observes signs or symptoms and begins to wonder if there's a reasonable suspicion of child abuse.

After meeting with the child safety committee, if a volunteer or staff with firsthand information still believes there is a suspicion of child abuse, he or she should report the matter immediately to police officials or a child protection agency. Even if the child safety committee does not concur with the volunteer or staff, they may not prohibit the volunteer or staff from reporting a reasonable suspicion of abuse.

What to do?

Jason is the Scout leader for a troop of eight- and-nine-year-old boys. While helping two boys clean up the workroom, Jason overhears Ben tell Luke that his dad hit him with a vacuum hose like the one Luke is using. Luke starts to laugh, but Jason is compelled to learn a little more about what happened. He asks Ben, "When did that happen?" Ben shrugs his shoulders and said it happened last summer. "Well, what exactly happened?" asks Jason. Ben tells Luke and Jason that he was supposed to pick up his things and vacuum his room before his dad got home from the store. But when his dad returned, Ben had only begun to pick up. Ben said his dad got mad and grabbed the plastic hose attached to the vacuum cleaner. He hit Ben across the back and on the legs with it and told him to get busy and clean his room. Jason asks if he got hurt, and Ben again shrugs his shoulders. He says, "I didn't cry." Then Jason asks if it happened more than once. Ben replies, "Nope. Mostly my dad just spanks me with his hand." Jason asks, "How often is that, Ben?" Ben replies, "Not very often."

- Do you think there's a suspicion that Ben is being abused by his dad?
- If Jason is uncertain about making a report, what should he do?

Tip
It's important that volunteers, staff, or child safety committees do not use the consultation as a means to delay reporting or to dissuade someone from reporting a reasonable suspicion of child abuse.

Child safety committee members ordinarily should not file a report of suspected child abuse on behalf of another volunteer or staff. However, if the volunteer or staff with firsthand information is unwilling to file a report and committee members believe a reasonable suspicion of child abuse exists, then a committee member should file a report.

The duties of your child safety committee in a potential reporting situation include:

- Meeting with the volunteer or staff person who has questions about something he or she observed or heard that may be considered abusive.

- Notifying executive staff, senior staff, or a designated responder of the report the child safety committee has received, extending the notification step to the governing body or board members when the alleged abuser is also a volunteer or staff person or if the alleged incident occurred during one of the organization's programs.

- Notifying the organization's legal counsel and insurance agent when a volunteer or staff person reports suspected child abuse to police officials or to a child protection agency (when the alleged abuser is a volunteer or staff member of the organization or when the alleged abuse occurred in the organization's facilities or programs).

- Assigning a member of the committee or the organization to respond to the media when there is public disclosure of the report.

- Assigning a member of the committee or the organization to assist the alleged victim and his or her family. Whether an organization can assign staff or volunteers to help individuals harmed by abuse may depend on the organization, the advice of its legal counsel, the nature of the allegation, the progress or context of the investigation, and the family's desire for help from the organization.

- Assigning staff or volunteers to conduct an investigation into charges of child abuse, if deemed necessary. This should happen *only* if the abuse allegedly occurred in the organization's facility, during one of its programs, or by one of its staff members or volunteers. Investigating allegations of child abuse against family members and or investigating incidents that occur *outside* the organization's programs and facilities is not the domain of your organization's child safety committee.

Finally, staff and volunteers who work with youth should receive training on the signs and symptoms of neglect and emotional, physical, and sexual abuse. These signs and symptoms vary, ranging from the physical to the psychological. Training should also include awareness of family behaviors and attitudes as well as indicators of family dysfunction that could contribute to an abusive environment. (For further help see Appendix M, "Signs and Symptoms of Child Abuse.")

Check out these resources in your community and enlist their help in the training process: local police officials, local child protection agencies, community counseling agencies, community councils that target child abuse prevention, schools, pediatricians and pediatric nurse practitioners, social workers, and psychologists. Many nationwide organizations have personnel and resources available to provide education and training as well.

7 Understanding the Response Process

The Importance of a Response Policy

Proper reporting and proper responding are both essential. Both must be carried out with care and sensitivity. In each case of reported suspicion of abuse, it's critical to ask immediately how best to care for the allegedly abused child and family—and the alleged offender and family. As soon as the case investigation begins, response begins. And knowing how to best respond—to the alleged victim as well as the alleged abuser—is something your organization will need to know and practice.

It is not often easy. It can be quite difficult to offer care to alleged victims and their families. Sometimes the child and family may leave the organization or program, asking not to be contacted. Or, if the family or your organization consults legal counsel, either party may be advised to avoid contact with the other party until the investigation concludes. In some cases, membership in the organization keeps some family members connected while the victim or other family members stay away. Further, a sense of shame and distrust or an understandable desire for privacy may deter families from seeking care from the organization.

It's also difficult to offer care to the alleged offender and family. If the offender remains associated with the organization, the organization may have that opportunity; however, if the organization terminates the person's employment or the person chooses to leave, the opportunity to offer care is diminished.

Procedures for Responding

Here are some guidelines for helping your organization respond to different scenarios involving alleged abusers. If one scenario does not fit your particular situation, you may need to tailor a response policy that works best for you.

Tip
When an allegation of abuse arises, it's important that your organization gather all documents surrounding the allegation and place them in a locked file. Strictly limit access to the file to those designated to interact with police officials and child protection authorities. Only your governing body and any designated person should have the authority to allow access to materials in the file by your legal counsel or insurance carrier. You should presume that anyone else who gains access to it has breached confidentiality.

Procedures for Nonprofit Organizations
Responding to a volunteer or staff member who admits to abusing a minor

In this case, the alleged offender is a volunteer or staff member who has admitted abusing a minor who is not a relative. The alleged abuse happened in one of your organization's programs or facilities. Here's how you might respond:

- Report the admission or confirm that the admission was reported to police officials.

- Report the admission to your organization's governing body for adjudication of the matter.

- Either by adjudication or admission of abuse, remove the offender from his or her position and responsibilities. Suspend a staff person with pay or remove a volunteer pending further action.

- Following the results of a police investigation or an internal investigation, the governing body should dismiss the volunteer from the organization and terminate a paid employee from the organization. Your governing body should consult with legal counsel regarding the termination of a paid staff member.

- Terminated staff persons and dismissed volunteers should be barred from further service in their previous (or similar) capacity within that organization.

- The governing body should also notify the organization's constituency regarding the removal, dismissal, suspension, or termination of a volunteer or staff member.

Responding to a volunteer or staff member who denies abusing a minor

In this case, the alleged offender is a volunteer or staff member who denies the allegation of abuse of a minor who is not a relative. Again, the abuse happened in one of your programs or facilities. Here's how you might respond:

- Report the allegation or confirm that the alleged offense was reported to the police officials. Determine that the officials have begun an investigation.

- Bring the allegation (and the person's denial of it) to your organization's governing body for adjudication of the matter.

- The governing body should receive written documentation specifying the nature of the allegations and the information known at this point. They may give the accused an opportunity to confront the allegations.

- If the governing body learns that allegations of abuse merit serious investigation or if there is the possibility of formal charges, it should take at least one of the following steps:

  ▶ Supervise all contact between the accused and the accuser (and between the accused and all other minors, as well).

  ▶ Restrict contact between the accused and the accuser and other minors.

  ▶ Remove or suspend (with pay) the accused from his or her position or responsibilities pending the outcome of the investigation

- If the governing body learns that criminal charges were filed against the accused, it should restrict all contact with minors and remove or suspend the person from his or her position and responsibilities.

- If the governing body learns that criminal proceedings have concluded, it should revisit the matter and take appropriate action:

  ▶ If criminal charges have been dropped or the trial resulted in acquittal, the governing body should decide whether to rescind its earlier action.

  ▶ If the trial results in conviction, the abuser is subject to termination (if previously suspended) or dismissal (if previously removed). The organization should bar the abuser from further service in his or her previous position or similar capacity within that organization.

- The governing body should also notify the organization's constituency regarding the removal, dismissal, suspension, or termination of a volunteer or staff member.

Responding to a volunteer or staff member accused by a relative
In this case, the alleged offender is a staff person or volunteer who is related to the alleged victim. Here's how you might respond:

- Report the allegation or confirm that the allegation was reported to Children's Protective Services or Children's Aid Society. Determine that an investigation has begun.

- If the accused admits physical or sexual abuse of a relative who is a minor, bring the admission to the organization's governing body. The accused should be removed (volunteer) or suspended with pay (staff person) from any position or responsibilities pending further action.

- Pending the outcome of an investigation, the volunteer may be dismissed and the staff person terminated. The governing body should consult with legal counsel before terminating a person in a paid position.

- A volunteer or staff person who admits abusing a relative who is a minor should be barred from future service in his or her previous position or similar capacity within the organization.

- If the accused denies the abuse allegation, bring the written allegation to the governing body. The governing body should take at least one of the following steps:

    ▶ Supervise or restrict contact between the accused and other minors in the organization

    ▶ Remove (volunteer) or suspend with pay (staff) the accused pending the outcome of the investigation.

- If the accused is charged with a crime, the governing board should remove or suspend the person, pending the outcome of the trial.

- If the accused is later cleared of the allegations, the governing board should decide whether to rescind its earlier action.

- If the accused is convicted of the allegations, the governing board should dismiss the volunteer or terminate the staff person—with advice from legal counsel.

- A dismissed volunteer or terminated staff member is barred from future service in the previous position or similar capacity within the organization.

- The governing body should also notify the organization's constituency regarding the removal, dismissal, suspension, or termination of a volunteer or staff member.

Responding to an alleged offender who is not a staff member or volunteer

In this case, the alleged offender is a member of the organization, but *not* one of its staff members or volunteers. Here's how you might respond:

- Report the allegation or confirm that the allegation was reported either to a child protection agency (when the minor is a relative) or to police officials (when the minor is not a relative). Determine that an investigation has begun.

- If the alleged offender is a relative of the child or youth, the organization should not conduct an independent investigation.

- If the alleged offender is a not related to the alleged victim, the organization should not conduct an independent investigation but should cooperate with civil authorities in their investigation. Civil authorities may advise the organization to initiate steps to supervise or restrict contact between the alleged offender and minors who are part of the organization.

- Regardless of the relationship of the alleged offender to the alleged victim, that person should be denied volunteer or paid opportunities in the organization during the course of the investigation.

- Regardless of the relationship of the alleged offender to the alleged victim, if convicted of child abuse, that person should be barred from volunteer or paid opportunities in the organization.

Procedures for Faith-based Organizations

If your organization is a church, you should offer pastoral care and support services to the alleged victim, the alleged offender, and the family members of both. In addition, your church should address the congregation's concerns when allegations of abuse arise by or against one of its members. Here are some helpful guidelines:

Responding to allegations against a church member by a minor

- An admission of child abuse by a church member (whether or not the member is related to the victim) should be reported to the appropriate authorities. After confirming that a report has been made and officials have begun an investigation, the admission should come before the church's governing body.

- The church's governing body may proceed with steps of discipline—based on an admission of guilt—prior to the completion of a civil investigation or judicial proceedings.

- The governing body should bar the person from future opportunities for positions or responsibilities with children or youth and from positions of trust and authority in general.

- Even if the accused denies the allegation of child abuse, he or she should be denied volunteer or paid opportunities throughout the investigation process. (Based on the outcome of the investigation, this denial may be lifted or steps of discipline initiated.)

- The church should comply with any restrictions placed on a convicted offender by courts or civil authorities, including restrictions required by a probation officer or court-appointed counselor.

- The governing body should notify the congregation regarding the prosecution or conviction for child abuse of a general member.

Responding to allegations against a church leader by a minor

- When a church leader is accused of physical or sexual abuse by a minor, the allegation should be reported to a child protection agency (when the minor is a relative) or to the police (when the minor is not a relative).

- After confirming that an investigation has begun, the allegation should be brought before the church's governing body.

- The governing body should receive any written documentation specifying the nature of the allegation and the information known at this point. The governing body may give the church leader an opportunity to confront the allegation.

- If the alleged victim is a relative, and the leaders admits the abusive behavior, the following steps should be observed:

    ▶ The leader should be removed (volunteer) or suspended with pay (staff) from any position or responsibilities.

    ▶ Pending the outcome of an investigation or trial, the leader should be subject to steps of discipline including dismissal of a volunteer, termination of paid staff, or release from ministerial duties.

    ▶ The church leader should be barred from future service in the previous position or similar capacity and from a position of trust and authority within the church.

- If the alleged victim is a relative, and the church leader denies the allegation of abuse, consider the following:

    ▶ The governing body should restrict the church leader's duties and remove the leader as a volunteer or suspend the leader (with pay) from his or her staff position.

    ▶ Pending the outcome of the investigation or trial, the governing body should rescind its earlier decision or initiate steps of discipline, including removal or dismissal of a volunteer, suspension or termination of a paid staff, or release from ministerial duties.

- A convicted church leader should be barred from future service in the previous position or similar capacity and from positions of trust and authority within the church.

- When the alleged victim is not a relative of the alleged abuser and the person admits to the abuse, proceed in the same way as you would if the victim were a relative (see above).

- When the alleged victim is not a relative and the church leader denies the allegation, consider taking the following actions:

  ▶ The church's governing body should supervise or restrict all contact between the church leader and minors in the church's programs and facilities.

  ▶ They may choose to remove the volunteer or suspend (with pay) the staff from his or her position and responsibilities while the investigation is taking place.

  ▶ Pending the outcome of the investigation or trial, your church's governing body may rescind its earlier decision or initiate steps of discipline, including removal or dismissal of volunteers, suspension or termination of paid staff, or release from ministerial duties.

  ▶ A church leader who has been dismissed, terminated, or released from ministry should be barred from future service in a previous position or similar capacity and from positions of trust and authority within the church.

- The governing body should also notify the congregation regarding the removal, dismissal, suspension, or termination of a volunteer or staff member, as well as release from duties of ministerial staff.

Responding to an alleged victim who is now an adult
Your church or organization may encounter an adult who alleges an incident of abuse that happened when he or she attended one of your programs as a child or youth. In this case, your organization's response will depend on whether or not the accuser remains connected to your organization. If the alleged abuser remains a part of the organization or church, then steps must be taken to learn more and respond appropriately. If the alleged abuser is no longer a part of the organization or church, a different approach must be taken.

In the first scenario, your organization will want to learn more about the alleged victim's story and determine the potential risk to any children or youth who may currently be under the alleged offender's care or authority. If any suspicion arises, contact the police. Because the accuser is now an adult, he or she should contact the local police regarding their complaint. In the meantime, your church or organization should consult legal counsel while cooperating with the investigation. The status of the investigation will determine the next steps you should take—if the police are unable to investigate the claim (the statute of limitations may apply), the organization should conduct its own investigation.

You'll want to cooperate with any effort to identify other victims of the alleged abuser. Depending on the circumstances, you may also want to notify the constituency of the allegation, the investigation, and any civil claim.

In the second scenario (the alleged abuser is no longer part of the organization), your governing body should consult with legal counsel regarding the steps they may take to assist the alleged victim with an investigation—either locally or in the community where the alleged offender now resides. The organization should cooperate with the investigation as to when and where the alleged incident occurred, especially if it allegedly occurred during an organization's programs or in its facilities.

If the results of the investigation validate the alleged victim's story, the results of the investigation should be documented and placed in the former volunteer or staff's personnel file, or in a separate file if the personnel records have been removed or destroyed. Again, your organization should cooperate with any effort to identify other victims, and you should notify your constituency.

Disclosure to Parents and the Community

With the best interests of the alleged victim in mind, your church's or organization's governing body should notify the congregation or community in writing of the admission of wrongdoing by the offender. In doing so, you must protect the identity of the victim; however, the offender's name should be disclosed for the protection of other minors as well as members of your congregation or community. Such disclosure should not exceed the scope of the admission. In the absence of an admission of wrongdoing, such disclosure of alleged abuse should not attempt to draw any legal conclusions about the guilt or innocence of any person. In either event, it is important that the disclosure include both factual information and a pastoral or sensitive response to the parties and their respective families. Remember, too, that it is wisest to disclose to your congregation or constituents before the matter is made public by the media or by a highly visible arrest.

Similarly, your governing body should notify the congregation or community in writing when it removes, dismisses, suspends, or terminates a volunteer, staff member, or church leader from his or her position or responsibilities following allegations of child abuse. The congregation or community should be informed that this action remains in effect pending the outcome of the investigation. Again, do not identify the alleged victim in your communication. Written notification should not exceed the scope of the information known about the matter, nor attempt to draw any legal conclusions about the guilt or innocence of any person. (For further help, see Appendices K and L, sample letters to the congregation and the community.)

Establishing Media Guidelines

While a child safety policy goes a long way towards discouraging and reducing the risk of child abuse in your church or organization, it is not foolproof. An adult or older teenager with malevolent motives can find his or her way through a screening policy and find a place in the organization where he or she can harm a child and cause hurt to the child's family and the entire organization.

Organizations are justifiably afraid of an allegation of child abuse against one of its volunteers or staff members. When that happens, a cloud comes over the entire organization. When the community hears the news, it raises eyebrows, and the allegation soon moves from an internal matter to a community-wide entanglement.

Informing the media that your organization has knowledge of an abuse incident is critical. For the victim and the victim's family (though they should remain unnamed) it provides an open and honest acknowledgement that their story was believed. It also gives the organization's volunteers and staff a standard for accountability.

Communication with the media should be structured so that information is accurately communicated without harming the investigation or the parties involved. Public confirmation via the media allows the community to gauge the organization's honesty and forthrightness in dealing with the matter, as well as its promise to pursue the case with integrity.

Here are some suggestions for dealing with the media:
- Designate one spokesperson who will address the media.

- Suggest that your spokesperson always speak from written notes and decline to address issues he or she is not familiar with.

- Advise your spokesperson not to speculate or surmise, but to speak only about known facts in the situation.

- Take a non-defensive stand, telling the media what the organization knows and what it is doing to respond to the crisis.

- Speak of the future, informing the media how the organization intends to help the victim, the offender, the families involved, and the community and/or congregation deal with this event.

- Think and speak humbly. Placing blame is a petty and unhelpful response at a time like this, and a show of anger can be misinterpreted as directed towards the victim.

- Establish credibility by responding with "I don't have an answer to that" or "I've been advised not to address that" rather than saying "No comment."

(For more help, see Appendix J, "Suggested Media Disclosure Policy.")

Developing a Duty to Warn Policy

It seems fitting to end this handbook with conversation about a duty to warn policy. In previous chapters we've talked about *duty* as taking reasonable steps to reduce the risk of abuse to children and youth served by your organization.

Before we conclude, let's acknowledge one more *duty*—the duty to warn other organizations that someone who's currently involved with yours may pose a substantial risk of harm to children and youth. The duty shifts from protecting the youth in your organization to protecting the youth in other organizations.

True, this additional duty comes with additional liability. The duty to warn carries with it the risk of slandering another person or causing injury to his or her reputation. The information an organization obtains about a person in question must be *actual* knowledge—not rumor, gossip, or innuendo. It's also important to discern that there is indeed a substantial risk of harm to other children and youth in the organizations you intend to warn.

If organizations like yours implement comprehensive child safety policies, a convicted sexual offender will find it difficult to move from organization to organization without detection. However, the offender who resigned from an organization rather than face adjudication has considerable more freedom to move around without detection, particularly when organizations fail to take seriously their duty to warn. Lest anyone think that liability rests only on an organization for transmitting information to another organization, you should know that there is also risk of liability to an organization that fails to warn or pass along actual knowledge of substantial risk of harm to children to those who need to know.

Tip
The most obvious opportunity to communicate helpful information about someone who presents a threat to children is when that person asks for a reference for a position with a different organization. Federal employment laws provide greater protection to paid employees than to volunteers when sharing information regarding an employee's conduct and performance. To balance the dual concerns of protecting children *and* protecting a person's reputation from reckless maligning, consult legal counsel.

A Appendix

Preventing Bullying: The Church's Obligation

"Bullying is aggressive behavior that is intentional and that involves an imbalance of power or strength. Typically it is repeated over time."

"What we know about bullying," a publication of U.S. Department of Health and Human Resources

"Bullying is aggressive or intentionally harmful behavior that is carried out repeatedly over time in an interpersonal relationship characterized by an imbalance of power."

PREVNet

Bullying seems to be the issue of the day. One can hardly open a newspaper, magazine, or school bulletin without noticing an article related to the problem of children abusing other children. Dr. Dan Olweus, a professor at the University of Bergen in Norway, has done pioneering work in this field since the 1980s. He began studying the issue after three separate incidents of schoolboys committing suicide; the victims had all been the subjects of chronic bullying. Subsequent studies have confirmed the prevalence of bullying as well as its lifelong effects in the lives of children it touches.

Bullying can have major social, educational, health, and other implications for children who bully, who are bullied, or who witness the bullying of others.

Children who are bullied have higher rates of suicide, depression, and substance abuse. They may begin carrying weapons to protect themselves. Bullied children may begin skipping school and doing poorly academically. A study conducted by the U.S. Secret Service and the U.S. Department of Education to investigate the causes and prevention of violent attacks on schools found that "almost three-quarters of the attackers felt

Much research on bullying has been done worldwide in the last twenty years. Statistics vary, but researchers agree that bullying is a universal problem. All statistics and findings reported in this article are derived from these sources:

- U.S. Department of Health and Human Services, through its web page http://www.stopbullyingnow.hrsa.gov. The department has a huge data bank of information available in PDF format, with sources and studies cited for all its statistics. It is also the sponsor of the Stop Bullying Now program.

- PREVNet—Promoting Relationships and Eliminating Violence Network (www.prevnet.ca) PREVNet comprises thirty-one Canadian researchers and thirty-nine national non-government organizations who share a commitment to working to promote healthy relationships for children and youth. The directors of PREVNet are leading researchers Dr. Debra Pepler of York University, Toronto, and Dr. Wendy Craig of Queen's University, Kingston. PREVNet carries downloadable studies and resources on its website.

- Research compiled by Dr. Olweus for his Bullying Prevention Program, found in *Blueprints for Violence Prevention, Book Nine: Bullying Prevention Program* by Dan Olweus, Sue Limber, and Sharon Mihalic, published in 1999. An abstract of this book can be found at http://www.ncjrs.gov/App/Publications/abstract.aspx?ID=174202.

persecuted, bullied, threatened, attacked, or injured by others prior to the incident" (*Safe Schools Initiative Final Report*, May 2002). Hopeless and helpless victims of bullying may commit suicide as a last resort.

Bullying also hurts bullies. Olweus found that students (particularly boys) who bully others are especially likely to engage in other antisocial or delinquent behaviors such as vandalism, shoplifting, truancy, and frequent drug use. As young adults, former school bullies had a fourfold increase in the level of relatively serious, recidivist criminality as documented in official crime records. Because they have learned negative and violent relational patterns, they often have difficulty forming and maintaining friendships and marriages later in life. Bullies who feel threatened may use their perceived power to strike out in violent ways, hurting others.

And those who witness bullying are also affected. They often feel guilty and helpless because they are too scared to stop a bullying incident. Some deal with these feelings of guilt by blaming the victim, deciding that he or she deserved the abuse. They may also end a friendship or avoid being seen with the bullied child to avoid losing status or being targeted themselves. If a child observes bullying behavior going unchecked, he or she may regard bullying behavior as acceptable. Over time, such episodes can result in harsher, less empathetic social climates, which foster new bullying episodes and other problems

Bullying at Church: Is It an Issue?

Although you may agree that bullying is a serious issue, perhaps you wonder why the church should get involved with its prevention. After all, children spend far fewer hours in church than at school or socializing with their peers.

PREVNet's comments (see sidebar) do not include churches in this list of community social agencies. However, the church is part of the community, and as such, should be an important part of the solution to bullying. But more importantly, bullying is not first of all a physical, mental, social, or educational issue. It's at heart a spiritual issue—bullying is about treating people as things, rather than as imagebearers of God. God created humankind for life-giving relationships with him and with the rest of our fellow creatures. Bullying behavior, wherever it occurs, turns that intent upside-down. Bullying is about violence against and contempt for others. It creates a climate of fear, alienation, insecurity, and suspicion—negative emotions that inhibit the formation of healthy self-concepts, loving relationships, and strong community.

"Bullying is a community problem, not a school problem. Bullying does not unfold alone in isolated islands of peers, families, or even schools. It exists in a much larger context. We have come to understand bullying as a community problem because bullying occurs in all contexts where people—not just children—come together to work and play. Bullying can happen at home, at the mall, in the hockey arena, and at the park.

"As the primary institution and a major socialization force in children's lives, schools...do play a leadership role in addressing bullying problems.... Schools, however, cannot be expected to address this social problem alone. In efforts to reduce bullying, schools need the supportive attitudes and responses of all systems in which children live: at home, in sports and extracurricular activities, in recreation centers, in the neighborhood and in the larger society, including the media."

From PREVNet's report, "Binoculars on bullying: a new solution to protect and connect children" Feb. 2007.

The church is the body of Christ, a community of believers, but bullying tears holes in that fabric of relationships, both with God and with others.

On a deeper level, an incident of bullying in a child's life may become a "funding event." Funding events are emotionally charged incidents that provide powerful images with long-lasting significance. They may shape our interpretation of life as we try to make sense of the present. "The funding events of our lives, those deep places of meaning and self-understanding, tend to stay with us for a lifetime...and can become places of entrapment and stagnation," says Ronald Cram in his book *Bullying: a Spiritual Crisis*. He goes on to say, "The energy, both positive and negative, produced by funding events can last many years or even a lifetime." Bullying—for the bully, the bullied and the bystander—can become such a funding event, shaping a child's perception of God and the Christian community. Bullying that takes place within the confines of the church community, whether in Sunday school, youth groups, midweek programs, at worship, or in fellowship halls, may have serious and long-lasting spiritual consequences.

Jesus said, "If any of you put a stumbling-block before one of these little ones who believe in me, it would be better for you if a great millstone were fastened around your neck and you were drowned in the depth of the sea" (Matthew 18:6, NRSV). In *The Message*, Eugene Petersen phrases it this way: "But if you give them a hard time, bullying or taking advantage of their simple trust, you'll soon wish you hadn't...Doom to the world for giving these God-believing children a hard time! Hard times are inevitable, but you don't have to make it worse." When the church turns a blind eye on bullying or denies its existence, it may be throwing a stumbling-block before the little ones.

Because many children never report bullying or believe that reporting will only make the matter worse, those who've been hurt by bullying behavior within the walls of the church may quietly drop out of your programs, never to hear God's healing message of love or experience reconciliation with the body of Christ.

Little work has been done by churches to address bullying. In 2005, the Presbyterian Church in Canada called together an ecumenical roundtable, the Canadian Ecumenical Anti-Bullying Initiative (CEABI), to investigate possible roles the Christian community might assume in confronting the problem of bullying. CEABI's definition of bullying adds a *spiritual* dimension: "Bullying is repeated behavior with negative intent that causes harm, intimidation or distress. It seeks to establish a relationship through misuse of power. It demonstrates contempt and excludes individuals from community. Bullying threatens the possibility of life-giving relationships and is a sign of spiritual crisis."

Recognizing Bullying Behavior

Bullying behavior falls into these categories, though the list is not all-inclusive.

Verbal bullying can be seen in taunting, name-calling, belittling, defamation, racial slurs, sexually abusive or suggestive remarks, malicious nicknames, extortion, abusive phone calls, gossip, or making a child the butt of jokes.

Verbal bullying accounts for about 70 percent of reported bullying incidents and is perpetrated equally by girls and boys. It plays a large part in relational bullying (see below) and is not always easy to detect, especially when whispering and gossip are part of the mix. Over time, repeated verbal bullying can break the spirit of a vulnerable child and damage fragile self-esteem. If verbal bullying is not stopped, it can escalate into physical and relational bullying.

Physical bullying is evidenced by hitting, punching, kicking, shoving, tripping, slapping, choking, biting, scratching, twisting limbs into painful positions, spitting, and damaging clothes or property. This kind of bullying is the most visible, but accounts only for about one-third of all bullying incidents. Bullies may excuse themselves by saying, "I didn't mean to hurt him; it was an accident." Children who engage in this kind of behavior are more likely to move on to more serious criminal behavior.

Although physical bullying in the past was mostly perpetrated by boys, recent statistics show that girls are engaging in this behavior more and more, driven by society's message that "girls can do anything that boys can do."

Relational bullying is seen in shunning, ignoring, isolating, excluding, and spreading rumors, lies, or gossip to diminish the social standing of the bullied child. These actions are often accompanied by subtle gestures such as eye-rolling, sighs, frowns, sneers, snickers, and hostile body language. This behavior, more common in girls than in boys and often conducted by groups or cliques, is the most difficult to detect. It systematically diminishes a bullied child's sense of self.

Cyber bullying is a sub-category of verbal and relational bullying and the newest entree into the world of bullying. It uses the latest technological tools to hurt others: e-mail, blogs, text messages, cell phones, chat rooms, and so on. It can be extremely damaging and have devastating results on the target. A simple rumor can be multiplied a thousand times in minutes; an unflattering or compromising picture taken on a cell-phone can reach around the world via the Internet; anonymous threats can arrive in an e-mail inbox, leaving the victim terrorized by an unknown aggressor.

Legal Implications of Bullying

As awareness of the problem grows and as more research is done into the long-term consequences of bullying, the issue will come into clearer legal focus. At the time of this writing it is hard to find clear definitions and legal precedents for dealing with bullying. In *Bullies, Targets and Witnesses*, SuEllen Fried, a leading anti-bullying advocate, writes, "We believe that identifying bullying...as a form of child abuse is the number-one challenge. Until the cruelty of children to each other is taken as seriously as the cruelty of adults to children, the issue will never receive its due attention" (p. 249-50).

Generally, the laws against harassment serve to cover bullying incidents. For instance, in 2002, a teenager was convicted in British Columbia of criminal harassment for verbally threatening a schoolmate who subsequently committed suicide. A week later, the BC Human Rights Tribunal held the North Vancouver School Board responsible for the impact of bullying and homophobic harassment. It awarded compensation to a young man who had been physically assaulted, spat upon, taunted, and harassed by other students because of his perceived sexual orientation.

However, there are differences between harassment and bullying. Harassment guidelines, definitions, and laws have originated out of governments' establishment of human and civil rights codes to prevent discrimination. Harassment laws exist on various levels to prevent discrimination on the basis of gender, race, ethnic background, color, religion or belief, sexual orientation, or disability. Harassment may be a single incident or a series of incidents, and it may not always be associated with intent. Also, it may occur in a situation where there is not an imbalance of power.

Bullying behavior, on the other hand, as we have seen in the definitions above, is marked by intention, repetition, and an imbalance of power (or a perceived imbalance of power). Discrimination may not be part of the motivation—the target just happens to be in the wrong place at the wrong time. Bullying carries with it an element of emotional violence that can have a profound impact on impressionable young psyches.

At the time of this writing, 36 states in the United States have passed legislation dealing with bullying in school situations, and a dozen more are working on it. (See www.bullypolice.org for the latest information.) Often, as in Vermont's Bill H629, the bullying legislation is an addition to an existing bill on harassment. The contents of these laws include some or all of the following stipulations: to require school officials to develop anti-bullying policies; to institute training on bullying for their employees; to require individuals to report school bullying incidents to authorities; to discipline children who bully; and to improve communication among staff and students related to bullying. While at this time these laws apply to schools only, it is possible that in the future and as awareness grows, as was the case with child abuse legislation, bullying legislation will change to apply to other community situations.

Facts about Bullying

Most statistics on bullying are gathered from studies done at schools rather than at churches. This may be a reflection of the fact that churches often lag behind other institutions in acknowledging social problems that may affect its members—for example, society at large acknowledged the reality and harmful effects of spousal and child abuse long before churches did.

Ronald Cram, author of *Bullying: A Spiritual Crisis*, writes, "Yet while public interest and research attention around the globe have begun to focus in intentional ways on the issue of bullying, virtually no ongoing research on bullying exists within the field of Christian religious education. But the church or the parish is exactly where the topic of bullying needs to be talked about and explored....For Christian people, violence is a matter of enormous theological concern" (Preface p. xiii and p. 2).

This does not mean that statistics about bullying are meaningless for the church. As PREVNet states, bullying is not primarily a school problem, it is a community problem, a relational problem. If bullying occurs in school classrooms, we may expect that it also happens in Sunday school classrooms; if it's occurring in children's clubs and sports teams, we may expect that it will also happen in church midweek clubs, youth groups, children's choirs, and youth team service projects. While the statistics printed below are mostly gathered from school situations, you can assume that the same things are happening in your church.

The following facts and figures, drawn from the resources listed at the beginning of this article, underline the serious nature of bullying:

- A child is bullied once every seven minutes on any given school playground, and once every twenty-five minutes in class (Pepler, et al, 1997).

- Nearly one in six children reports being victimized by bullies more than once or twice in the past six weeks.

- Peers are involved in some capacity in 85 percent of bullying episodes, and 48 percent of those involved actively take part in the bullying.

- Peers are significantly more likely to be respectful of bullies than of victims (74 percent supported the bullies).

- Physical bullying peaks at ages eleven or twelve, but persists into high school; verbal and relational bullying is more constant.

- Adults believe they intervene more than they actually do. In one study, 70 percent of teachers said adults "almost always" intervene to stop bullying—only 25 percent of students agreed.

- Twenty-five percent of teachers see nothing wrong with bullying or putdowns, and consequently intervene in only 4 percent of bullying incidents.

- Many children do not report incidents of bullying because they fear that telling adults will only bring more harassment from bullies. They also believe that adults do little or nothing to help in bullying incidents.

- Teachers' and leaders' attitudes, behaviors, and routines play a large role in the prevalence of bullying behavior; they are also integral to successful anti-bullying programs.

Bullying is a pervasive, serious problem that affects many children and teens, and which has serious consequences. Caring adults, however, can make a difference!

Examples of Bullying at Church

Not all misbehavior can be construed as bullying. Bullying has three markers:

- It's intentional.

- It's repeated.

- It involves an imbalance of power.

Consider the following vignettes:

Scenario 1: Kevin is a conscientious and enthusiastic member of a boy's midweek club. But one day he arrives at class with a scrape on his face, a hole in his jeans, and no badge work in hand. (He tells the leader that he left it at home.) Meanwhile, Jimmy and Thomas present an excellent project they say they worked on together. The leader is surprised: these two boys are generally goof-offs. In the following weeks, Kevin misses a number of classes and eventually drops out of the program.

Points to Ponder:

- Kevin may or may not be the victim of Jimmy and Thomas's bullying. It's possible Kevin's home circumstances have changed for the worse, accounting for the dishevelment and changed attitude.

- If Jimmy and Thomas took Kevin's project by force, but it's the first and only time they have intimidated him or others, it constitutes misbehavior.

- If, however, the boys show a pattern of intimidation and physical violence, they can be considered bullies.

- Kevin did not tell the leader the real reason he was without his project. Notice that if Jimmy and Thomas did take Kevin's project, it was done outside the meeting, outside the leader's view. It's not always easy to detect bullying.

Scenario 2: The youth leader has taken her junior high kids out for a weekend campout. Later, as she drops off Maria and Janelle at their homes, she tells them how much she's enjoyed it. As she drives away, Amy, the last person left in the car, remarks, "You thought that went well? Did you know that Maria and Janelle decided not to say a word to Sharma all weekend, even though she slept in their tent? They got almost all the other girls to treat her that way too, to teach Sharma a lesson—because they saw her talking to Maria's boyfriend. Sharma had a rotten weekend!"

Points to Ponder:

- Maria and Janelle have a position of power, as evidenced by their ability to influence others.

- Their actions were intentional; their goal was to isolate Sharma until she behaved according to their expectations.

- The leader was not aware of the difficult social situation for Sharma.

- Amy, who is uncomfortable with the situation, does not bring up the issue to the leader's attention while it is in progress; to do so could isolate her from her peers as well.

- If Maria and Janelle are not held accountable for their actions, they may believe that this is acceptable behavior, and may well fall into a pattern of relational bullying.

Scenario 3: Carlos is complaining again that he doesn't want to go to Sunday school. This time his mother resolves to get to the bottom of the problem, so she questions him until he expresses his feelings. He's concerned about his two friends in the class. He says that the teacher is picking on them all the time, making fun of them if they don't know the answers to questions by rolling his eyes and commenting sarcastically. Carlos is worried that he will be the next victim.

Points to Ponder:

- Bullying (intentional, repeated aggression by a person with greater power) is not only done by children. Adults can be bullies, too.

- Victims of bullying aren't the only ones harmed; children who observe bullying behavior are also affected by it.

- Carlos is reluctant to report his feelings to an adult but exhibits symptoms of distress.

- Church classrooms and meeting places should be safe places where children are respected regardless of their abilities

- If Carlos is feeling unsafe, the situation deserves to be investigated, either to clear his teacher's name and restore a good relationship with Carlos, or to confirm Carlos's perceptions.

Scenario 4: Jarod has energy to burn and a need for attention. He has a nickname for Matteo, who was born in Mexico—Taco. He tells his friends, strictly in secret of course, that Andre, who has rebuffed his friendship, might be a fag. In the hallway on the way to class, he extorts the collection money from Eva, who is small and shy. If caught in the act by his Sunday school teacher, he is always apologetic, although he always has an excuse or a reason: "I'm just teasing," or "I didn't mean to do that; it was an accident." Andy, his teacher, is baffled; he wonders how to deal with this child. Should he give him a taste of his own medicine, let him see what it feels like to be pushed around and humiliated?

Points to Ponder:

- Jarod is the classic example of a bully, someone who uses his power intentionally and repeatedly to harm others.

- Bullies often use excuses or blame the victim so they won't be held accountable for their actions.

- Racial and sexual bullying are part of the spectrum of relational bullying

- The teacher's solution is no solution, since it perpetuates the violence. However, his desire to stop the bullying is a step in the right direction.

- Jarod's need for attention is a key to understanding and changing the bullying behavior. Bullying is a learned behavior, and it *can* be unlearned.

- Bullies need to be held to account by practicing the three R's: *restitution*—apologizing and righting the wrong; *resolution*—figuring out a way to prevent the incident from happening again; and *reconciliation*—going through a process of healing the relationship between the bully and the victim.

Myths about Bullying

Myth: Bullies suffer from insecurity and low self-esteem. They pick on others to make themselves feel more important.
The research shows: Bullies may have low, average, or above-average self-esteem. Their behavior stems not from lack of self-esteem but from aggressive temperaments, a lack of empathy, and/or poor parenting. Bullies lack the ability to put themselves in someone else's shoes, to feel their pain. Bullies learn their behavior through observation and experience. The good news is that learned behavior can be unlearned.

Myth: If only victims of bullies learned to stand up for themselves and deal with the situation, the problem would go away.
The research shows: While there are strategies that bullied children can use to minimize the likelihood of an encounter with a bully, this will not stop bullying behavior. Victims of bullies are usually younger or physically weaker than their attackers. They may also lack the social skills to develop supportive friendships. They cannot deal with the situation themselves. They need adults on their side who know what to do.

Myth: Bullying is not a problem in my class (group, church, fellowship). I would know about it.
The research shows: There is virtually no bully-free zone in places where children gather. Bullying behavior usually takes place out of sight of teachers and leaders. Most victims are reluctant to report the bullying for fear of embarrassment or retaliation, and most bullies deny or justify their behavior. Denial of the issue only perpetuates the problem.

Myth: There is no law against bullying, so it must not be such a serious problem. All the attention paid to this issue is overblown.
The research shows: Most states have passed laws regarding bullying. The majority of the laws deal with the responsibility of schools to provide a safe place for children to learn. They also often make

provisions for intervention and counseling. Some states are now making it mandatory to report incidents of bullying to law enforcement agencies. Also, the consequences of bullying can be very serious, resulting in real physical harm and even death. In these instances, bullies, even children, will be charged with more serious crimes such as assault, aggravated harm, and murder. There are laws against harassment and abuse, which are really dressed-up forms of bullying.

Myth: The church is not the place to address this societal problem. And even if the church wanted to get involved, children are at church for such few hours a week, it could have only a minimal effect.
The research shows: As noted earlier, bullying is not just a school or societal problem, it is also a spiritual problem, and, as such, churches have a calling to address it. When churches address the issue, they can expect God to bless the work they do. Studies have shown that schools and other organizations with strong anti-bullying policies can significantly lower the incidence of bullying behavior.

How Can the Church Address Bullying?
Prevent bullying from happening in your church
Actions speak louder than words. All the anti-bullying policies in the world are useless unless people who work with children in church are good role models of healthy relationships. Ensuring that leaders in children and youth programs are caring models of Jesus' love is the first and most basic step a church should take.

In addition, education committees, staff, teachers, and children's program leaders need to be informed about this issue and how to deal with it. Training is essential because some adults still do not accept that bullying is a problem—or that it happens in church (see facts and figures, above). Without a clear understanding of the issue, leaders of children's programs are likely to ignore problems. (See Appendix C for a fact sheet you can give to your volunteers and staff to help raise their awareness.)

You can also find a great deal of printed information that staff and volunteers can read on their own or as a group. (See resource list in Appendix B; Barbara Coloroso's book, *The Bully, the Bullied and the Bystander* is a good introduction to the issue.) It's also very likely that speakers are available in your community to present a workshop or an information evening—contact your local school board or community health organization for more information.

Also falling under the heading of prevention is teaching practical coping strategies to children who may be victims or bystanders (those who witness the bullying but don't know how to intervene). A short piece in a book such as this one cannot cover the subject of bullying with any degree of thoroughness. The resources (Appendix B) can help your church learn more about taking these practical steps. While much of the material available is addressed to schools and parents, staff and volunteers in a church setting should also be equipped to give good advice when the topic of bullying arises.

Teachers and leaders of children's groups can do a lot to lessen the prevalence of bullying behavior. Remember, much of the bullying happens outside the classroom, so simple steps such as adequately supervising hallways, buses, and outings can make it more difficult for bullies to act. Holding bullies accountable for their actions by following the three R's (restitution, resolution, and reconciliation) also shows children that bullies won't get away with their behavior.

Church leaders can do a lot to raise awareness of bullying and promote healthy discussion and behavior. Sermons, discussion groups, information evenings, library resources, and book studies are just some of the ways to let your congregation know that bullying is a serious issue, and that victims can find a safe refuge within your church walls.

The committee responsible for ensuring safety within the church needs to consider and address this issue in a more formal way. You may decide to write a policy and establish procedures to follow when bullying is reported. An effective document should include the following:

- A statement of the church's stand against bullying.

- A succinct definition of bullying, including illustrations.

- A theological rationale for taking action against bullying.

- A statement of the responsibilities of all those who observe bullying to seek to stop it.

- A general description of how the church will deal with bullying incidents.

- A plan for evaluating the policy in the near future (specify time frame).

Arriving at policies and developing procedures that address bullying cannot be done in isolation. An effective anti-bullying strategy must be developed in community, with input from many members. It will be accompanied by awareness-raising and consultation, which helps people understand the problem and agree to a definition of bullying.

"Regardless of how these supports are put in place, one overarching principle is clear: children depend on adults to help them understand bullying problems and to promote the development of essential social skills, social perceptions, and social responsibility."

From PREVNet's report, "Binoculars on bullying: a new solution to protect and connect children" Feb. 2007.

Once the policy has been written, it must be clearly articulated, broadly communicated, and consistently enforced. The policy must be supported by a caring and warm environment—a church culture that values each child.

For more information on creating and writing an anti-bullying policy in your church and for a sample policy, contact the office of Abuse Prevention at (616) 224-0735 or swagmanb@crcna.org.

Ensure that the church is a safe place of healing and spiritual growth
Children who have been bullied often grow up to be hurting adults with relational problems. These adult victims of bullying, as well as hurting children who have been bullied, need a safe place to land, a place where people will listen to their stories, respect them, and help them recover and grow. What better place for them to come than to Christ's body, the church?

Church leaders should ask themselves these questions:
* Is there a safe place made available or opportunity extended so that victims can tell their stories?

* Are there people trained and willing to help victims heal, to whom the victim can be referred? (This may be a Christian counselor or agency outside the church, or a healing ministry within the congregation.)

* Is there a protocol to follow to hold bullies accountable if they are members of the congregation?

Answering these questions and ensuring that a protocol is in place to deal with hurting individuals goes a long way to showing people Jesus' love. Just as important, is the need that bullies, too, have for healing and spiritual growth. Their view of others is a distorted picture of God's created order. They have no respect for the image of God created within each person, and they do not understand that each person is an important part of Christ's body. Their view of relationships is based on power and dominance rather than mutuality. Surely, the church has a message of healing and growth for the bully as well.

Nurture empathy
Almost all studies that try to determine the root cause of bullying agree that bullies lack empathy. The quality of empathy allows a person to enter into and identify with another person's feelings. It's the ability to imagine what it's like to be in the predicament of the other person and, as a result, the ability to communicate that awareness so the other person feels understood. Bullies lack this quality.

How can the church help bullies to develop this Christlike compassion? You cannot teach empathy in the same way that you can teach knot-tying or gourmet cooking—by following step-by-step instructions. Empathy is "caught" more than "taught." It's learned through experience, observation, and teaching strategies that encourage a child to look within and reflect on his or her own heart condition. Consider these important ways of nurturing empathy:

- *Listen actively*: Teachers and leaders who really listen and give feedback to those who talk or tell their stories encourage children to think more deeply about issues. Questions such as, "How did that make you feel?" or "I wonder why someone would do such a thing?" or "What could you do to make your friend feel happier or better?" can stimulate a child to identify with others' feelings and thoughts.

- *Practice positive discipline with a bully*: The word discipline has as its root the word for "to learn." Discipline is not primarily about punishment but more about teaching new and better ways of behaving. The process of discipline helps bullies identify what they have done wrong, gives them ownership of the problem, helps them develop a process for solving the problem, and leaves their dignity intact.

- *Emphasize the three R's with bullies*:

  ▶ Restitution—fixing what they did, such as paying for a broken toy, giving back the extorted money, apologizing for the malicious words.

  ▶ Resolution—figuring out a way to keep it from happening again, such as counting to ten when they're angry or recognizing the stimulus that causes the bullying behavior, and deciding on a better coping mechanism.

  ▶ Reconciliation—finding a way to heal the broken relationship.

- *Practice warm Christian love*: Teachers and leaders are living examples of Jesus' love who model empathy when they give affection to children in appropriate ways and are helpful, polite, and interested in the children's personal lives.

- *Spotlight feelings*: Questions about feelings can be a part of every session; children can be encouraged to imagine the feelings of Bible characters or to voice their feelings about stories they hear or events they experience. Teachers and leaders should not feel as though they need to "fix" feelings as soon as they are expressed; allow children to be honest and help them work through to the positives.

- *Role-play*: Role play is an excellent teaching strategy that helps children identify with the feelings and ideas of others. A word of caution: warm up to role plays by involving the group in discussion along lines like these, for example: "One of the characters in this role play has just been in a minor fender-bender. What thoughts are running through his head as he jumps out of his car to inspect the damage?" Once children are well into imagining the scenario, assign roles for role play.

- *Encourage journaling or writing exercises* that focus on another person's perspective (for example, What did the little boy who gave his lunch to Jesus tell his mom when he came home?).

- *Teach about real-life people* who modeled empathy, and how this empathy resulted in great things: Nelson Mandela, Mother Teresa, Martin Luther King, and so on.

- *Use service projects*, especially real-life hands-on work with people who live with disabilities or poverty. Often bullies believe they are entitled to whatever they wish; working for others and learning about their lives often gives us new attitudes about ourselves.

- *Practice empathetic reactions*: Present a hypothetical problem situation a child might encounter (for example, a friend's parents have divorced or another friend's grandmother is dying). Discuss these questions together:

  ▶ What's the bad thing that happened?

  ▶ How is this person feeling about what happened?

  ▶ What can I do in response?

- *Praise positive behavior*: Catch kids doing good and reinforce that behavior, instead of harping on the negatives.

- *Provide opportunities for fellowship and friendship*: Parties, celebrations, projects, eating together, pen-pal relationships, and other such relational activities are warm and nurturing antidotes to negatives, and may fill up the holes in both a bully's and a target's life.

Want to read (and do) more about the issue of bullying? Check out the resource list in Appendix B.

Thanks to Jessie Schut for writing this appendix. Jessie Schut is a writer and church education consultant. She represented the Christian Reformed Church on the Canadian Ecumenical Anti-Bullying Initiative, a working study group convened by the Presbyterian Church in Canada in 2005.

B Appendix

Further Resources for Dealing with Bullying

For Teachers and Leaders:

Websites:
Literally hundreds of websites deal with this issue. The ones we've found most reputable and most helpful for general information, with links to dozens of resources, are:

- www.stopbullyingnow.hrsa.gov

- www.prevnet.ca

Books:
- *Bullying: A Spiritual Crisis* by Ronald H. Cram. Chalice Press, St. Louis, Missouri, 2003. ISBN 0-8272-0234-2

    There exists precious little information written from a Christian viewpoint on this subject. This book is the exception. It is written by a theology professor who looks at bullying as a spiritual crisis and places violence in a theological context. It arose out of his own experience of hearing stories from seminary students while teaching a class on Children's Spiritual Development. While not always an easy read, it serves as a good discussion starter for adult study groups and provides a clear spiritual framework for church policies and guidelines.

- *Bullies, Targets and Witnesses—helping children break the pain chain* by SuEllen Fried and Paula Fried. M. Evans and Company, New York, 2003. ISBN 1-59077-056-0

    This excellent book is a great introduction to the topic of bullying. Chapters give information on bullying in the 21st century, bullying statistics, the social context of bullying, strategies for students, parents, teachers, and educators to cope with bullying, legislation and policies, and challenges for the future.

- *And Words Can Hurt Forever* by James Garbarino and Ellen de Lara. The Free Press, New York, 2002. ISBN 0-7432-2898-7

    The subtitle of this book is "How to protect adolescents from bullying, harassment and emotional violence." It reviews the lethal impact emotional violence can have in the lives of adolescents, and examines causes of this violence. The book includes many facts and figures from studies and also interviews with teens who have experienced violence.

- *The Bully, the Bullied, and the Bystander* by Barbara Coloroso. Harper Collins, New York, 2002. ISBN 0-00-639420-5

  Aimed at parents and teachers, this book's goal is to help them break the cycle of violence. It gives a background and statistics to the topic of bullying, in-depth looks at the worlds of the bully, the bullied, and the bystander, and advice on how to create circles of caring that will break the cycle of violence.

- *The Wounded Spirit* (re-titled *No More Bullies*) by Frank Peretti. Thomas Nelson, 2000. ISBN 0-8499-4336-1

  Peretti is known for his spiritual thrillers, including *This Present Darkness*. In this book he tells his own story of growing up bullied, vividly describes the ensuing pain and scars, and challenges teens and adults to address this issue in their lives. An additional booklet, *No More Victims*, gives advice to teens on forming support groups and rooting out bullying in their social circles.

- *Risk in our Midst* by Dr. Scott Larson. Group Publishing, Inc., Loveland, Colorado, 2000. ISBN 0-7644-2248

  This book is aimed at leaders of Christian youth groups. It reminds leaders that there is a growing population of lost youth who are looking for friendship, hope, and caring. Will they find these qualities in your youth group or Sunday school class, or will they be rejected because they are "different"? The book shows leaders how to empower the teens in their group to show Jesus' love to the unlovable.

- *The Bully Free Classroom* by Allan L. Beane. Free Spirit Publishing, Minneapolis, 1999 (revised 2003). ISBN 1-57542-054-6

  This manual includes over one hundred tips and strategies for teachers of K-8 under the headings of Creating a Positive Classroom, Helping Victims, and Helping Bullies. As well, there are more than thirty reproducible pages that include questionnaires, worksheets for children, bullying facts and figures, tips for parents, and so on. The last twelve pages include a listing of agencies, websites, books, and other resources.

Workshop:

- *Bully for You*, a workshop in the TLC series for children's leaders, developed by the Presbyterian Church of Canada (also includes a resource kit). Search www.presbyterian.ca and check under Education in the Our Ministry section.

  Bullying is a problem that just doesn't seem to go away. Yet, bullying can be lessened with education, awareness, and good programs. Find out what resources and materials are available to help the children and youth in your Sunday school and community. Find out what churches can do to help with the issue of bullying. (Note: this workshop provides only a framework for presenters, who should be well-versed in the facts, figures, and possible solutions of this issue to provide the practical information.)

Film/Video:

- *It's a Girl's World*, National Film Board of Canada, 2002.
  [From NFB's description] *It's a Girl's World* takes us inside the tumultuous relationships of a clique of popular ten-year-old girls. Playground bullying captured on camera shows a disturbing picture of how these girls use their closest friendships to hurt each other—with shunning, whispering, and mean looks—to win social power in the group. Meanwhile, their parents struggle through denial and disbelief as they become aware of the serious consequences of this behavior. As well, it includes the tragic story of a fourteen-year-old girl, serving as a stark reminder that social bullying can spiral out of control. Believing she had no other choice, Dawn-Marie Wesley killed herself after enduring months of rumors and verbal threats. This documentary shatters the myth that social bullying among girls is an acceptable part of growing up.

The video also includes helpful extra clips to use in the classroom as discussions for children at different age levels.

For Children:

- *Safekeeping: Session Plans for Developing Abuse Awareness in Kids* by Henni Helleman and Patricia J. Vos. Faith Alive Christian Resources, Grand Rapids, Michigan, 2006.
  This package of materials provides two lesson plans at four different levels from kindergarten through 8th grade to develop abuse awareness in children. They are meant to be used in Sunday school classrooms, club meetings, or as stand-alone sessions that can be scheduled any time during the church education year. Besides hands-on discussion starters and activities, the package includes books that can also be read with the children. One session at grade 2-3 level, two sessions at the grades 4-5 level, and one session at the grade 6-8 level make specific references to bullying.

- *Bullies Are a Pain in the Brain* by Trevor Romain. Book and video published by Free Spirit Publishing, Minneapolis, 1997.
  Animated presentation about a child who is bullied and how he and his friend learn to deal with it. Defines bullies, dispels myths

about bullying (bullying is normal, bullies are always boys, and the best way to handle bullies is to ignore them or fight back), suggests positive coping and problem-solving strategies (stand tall and confident, stay calm, give bullies lots of space, tell an adult, use humor, plan your strategy, don't believe the bully, stick with friends). Fun and informative (for seven- to ten-year-olds).

- *Minnesota Cuke and the Search for Samson's Hairbrush* by Veggie Tales. Big Idea, a division of Sony Warner, 2005
  Popular, animated video presents a Christian view on dealing with bullies, including the message that God wants us to show love even to those who are unlovable. A hopeful ending (the bully and the bullied end up becoming friends) may be unrealistic for many bullying situations. A short extra features Junior Asparagus dealing with a real playground bully; the situation is resolved in part because Junior's friends stand up for him.

- *Bridge to Terabithia* by Katherine Paterson. HarperCollins, New York, 1977. A movie based on the book was released in 2007.
  This story, suitable for grade 4 and up, is written by Christian author Katherine Paterson. While not specifically about bullying, the issue is an important thread in the story. Reading parts of the book or viewing specific segments of the movie will serve as good discussion starters or journaling start points.

- *A Tale Worth Telling* by Linda Sky Grossman. Second Story Press, Toronto, 2002.
  David, the new boy, seems quiet and unfriendly. The other children discover that an adult (soccer coach) has made him feel bad about himself. He is worried that if he talks about it, no one will listen or believe him.

- *Let's Talk About Bullying* by Bruce S. Sanders. Stargazer Books (c/o The Creative company, Mankato, Minnesota), 2006.

- *Playground Survival* by Peggy Burns. Raintree (division of Reed Elsevier Books, Chicago, Illinois), 2005.

- *Stop Picking on Me—A First Look at Bullying* by Pat Thomas and Lesley Harker. Barron's Educational Series, 2003.

- *Bye-Bye, Bully! A Kid's Guide for Dealing with Bullies* by J.S. Jackson and illustrated by R.W. Alley. Abbey Press, St. Meinrad, Indiana, 2003.

- *Playing Fair, Having Fun—A Kid's Guide to Sports and Games* by Daniel Grippo and illustrated by R.W. Alley. Abbey Press, St. Meinrad, Indiana, 2004.

These books are good discussion starters for early elementary grades—they ask and answer common questions about bullying, and make practical helpful suggestions for how to deal with the issue.

- *Risk in Our Midst—Empowering Teens to Love the Unlovable* by Scott Larson. Group Publishing, Loveland, Colorado 2000.

  While the book itself addresses youth leaders, a section at the back provides a study guide for kids. A reviewer's quote from the Amazon.com website says, "We have started using this book in our youth group and found that it has put the finger on so many issues we were dealing with. The issues of teasing and bullying that were just part of our group are now being exposed through the six-part youth group series in the back of the book, and kids are taking ownership of it and wanting to change that. It's been awesome!"

- *The Bully and Me* by Helen Carmichael Porter. Northstone Press, Cleveland, 2006 (includes audio CD).

  This book of stories about bullying experiences explores the idea that victims and bullies are two sides of the same coin and that the healing of both lies in dealing with this paradox. The stories help readers recognize signs of bullying and provide conversation starters. Parents, educators, children, and youth can learn together how to cope in various situations. At the end of each story, Porter provides activities and questions for discussion.

Appendix

Bullying: A Fact Sheet for Teachers and Leaders of Children and Youth

What is bullying?

"Bullying is aggressive behavior that is intentional and that involves an imbalance of power or strength. Typically it is repeated over time."

"What we know about bullying"—a publication of U.S. Department of Health and Human Resources.

Note these three characteristics of bullying behavior:

- It is intentional.
- It is repeated.
- It involves an imbalance of power.

Why should I be concerned about bullying?

- Bullying is serious. Many studies have revealed major social, educational, health, and other implications for children who bully, who are bullied, or who witness bullying (see statistics printed below).
- Bullying, from a Christian perspective, is a spiritual issue. It's about treating people as things, rather than as imagebearers of God. Bullying is about violence against and contempt for others. It creates a climate of fear, alienation, insecurity, and suspicion—negative emotions that inhibit the formation of healthy self-concepts, loving relationships, and a strong community.

How prevalent is bullying?

While these statistics are derived from school studies, bullying behavior occurs wherever groups gather. You may assume that bullying statistics for church would be very similar to those found here:

- A child is bullied once every seven minutes on any given school playground, and once every twenty-five minutes in class (Pepler, et al, 1997).
- Nearly one in six children reports being victimized by bullies twice or more in the past six weeks.

- Peers are involved in some capacity in 85 percent of bullying episodes, and 48 percent of those involved actively take part in the bullying.
- Peers are significantly more likely to be respectful of bullies than of victims (74 percent supported the bullies).
- Physical bullying peaks at age eleven to twelve, but persists into high school; verbal and relational bullying is more constant.
- Adults believe they intervene more than they actually do. In one study, 70 percent of teachers said adults "almost always" intervene to stop bullying—only 25 percent of students agreed.
- Twenty-five percent of teachers see nothing wrong with bullying or putdowns, and consequently intervene in only 4 percent of bullying incidents.
- Many children do not report incidents of bullying because they fear that telling adults will only bring more harassment from bullies. They also believe that adults do little or nothing to help in bullying incidents.
- Teachers' and leaders' attitudes, behaviors, and routines play a large role in the prevalence of bullying behavior; they are also integral to successful anti-bullying programs.

How can I recognize bullying?

Verbal bullying: taunting, name-calling, belittling, defamation, racial slurs, sexually abusive or suggestive remarks, malicious nicknames, extortion, abusive phone calls, gossip, making a child the butt of jokes.

Physical bullying: hitting, punching, kicking, shoving, tripping, slapping, choking, biting, scratching, twisting limbs into painful positions, spitting, damaging clothes or property.

Relational bullying: shunning, ignoring, isolating, excluding, spreading rumors, lies or gossip to diminish the social standing of the bullied child. These actions are often accompanied by subtle gestures such as eye-rolling, sighs, frowns, sneers, snickers, and hostile body language.

Cyber bullying: using the latest technological tools such as e-mail, blogs, text messages, cell phones, chat rooms, and so on to hurt others (fast becoming a major issue).

What can teachers and leaders of children and youth do?

Prevent bullying from happening:

- Actions speak louder than words. Walk the walk. Be a caring model of Jesus' love.
- Learn all you can about bullying. A good place to start is one of the anti-bullying websites such as www.stopbullyingnow.hrsa.gov. Knowledge about the topic helps you be supportive of victims and

bystanders (those who witness the bullying but don't know how to intervene).

- Since bullying usually happens away from the teacher's view, be sure to adequately supervise hallways, buses, playgrounds, activities, and outings.
- Be observant and ask questions. Targets of bullying often become withdrawn, fear going outside, or withdraw from your program altogether.
- Hold a bully accountable for his actions by following the three R's (restitution, resolution, and reconciliation).
- Establish that your group meeting is a bully-free zone; involve your children/youth in setting guidelines for a healthy and safe meeting place.
- Follow policies and procedures recommended by your education/youth/ abuse prevention committees if and when you suspect that bullying is an issue for your group.

Help your church become a safe place of healing and spiritual growth.
- Become an active listener. Don't dismiss or shrug off stories about bullying.
- Affirm all children's strengths and frequently give positive feedback.
- Encourage children to share their stories, and encourage healthy group discussions.
- Be a peacemaker and a mender of broken relationships within your group.
- Hold bullies accountable so that you do not deepen the pain and hopelessness of the victim.
- Find out about resources your church may have (such as counseling referrals) that will help hurting children heal; guide them to seek out these resources.

Nurture empathy
The quality of empathy allows a person to enter into and identify with another person's feelings. People who empathize with others find it hard to bully.

Empathy is "caught" more than "taught." It is learned through experience, observation, and teaching strategies that encourage a child to look within and reflect on his or her own heart condition. As a teacher or leader of children in the church, you have a very unique opportunity to nurture this Christlike characteristic.

Consider these important ways of nurturing empathy:

- *Listen Actively*: Teachers and leaders who really listen and give feedback to those who talk or tell their stories encourage children to think more deeply about issues. Questions such as, "How did that make you feel?" or "I wonder why someone would do such a thing?" or "What could you do to make your friend feel happier or better?" can stimulate a child to identify with others' feelings and thoughts.

- *Practice positive discipline with a bully*: The word discipline has as its root the word for "to learn." Discipline is not primarily about punishment but more about teaching new and better ways of behaving. The process of discipline helps bullies identify what they have done wrong, gives them ownership of problem, helps them develop a process for solving the problem, and leaves their dignity intact.

- *Emphasize the three R's with bullies*:

  ▸ Restitution: fixing what they did, such as paying for a broken toy, giving back the extorted money, apologizing for the malicious words.

  ▸ Resolution: figuring out a way to keep it from happening again, such as counting to ten when they're angry or recognizing the stimulus that causes the bullying behavior and deciding on a better coping mechanism.

  ▸ Reconciliation: finding a way to heal the broken relationship.

- *Practice warm Christian love*: Teachers and leaders are living examples of Jesus' love. They model empathy and show Jesus' love when they give affection to children in appropriate ways and are helpful, polite, and interested in their personal lives.

- *Spotlight feelings*: Questions about feelings can be a part of every session; children can be encouraged to imagine the feelings of Bible characters or to voice their feelings about stories they hear or events they experience. Teachers and leaders should not feel as though they need to "fix" feelings as soon as they are expressed; allow children to be honest and help them work through to the positives.

- *Role-play*: Role play is an excellent teaching strategy that helps children identify with the feelings and ideas of others. A word of caution: warm up to role plays by involving the group in discussion along lines like these, for example: "One of the characters in this role play has just been in a minor fender-bender. What thoughts are running through his head as he jumps out of his car to inspect the damage?" Once children are well into imagining the scenario, assign roles for role play.

- *Encourage journaling or writing exercises* that focus on another person's perspective (for example, What did the little boy who gave his lunch to Jesus tell his mom when he came home?).

- *Teach about real-life people* who modeled empathy, and how this empathy resulted in great things: Nelson Mandela, Mother Teresa, Martin Luther King, and so on.

- *Use service projects*, especially real-life hands-on work with people who live with disabilities or poverty. Often bullies believe they are entitled to whatever they wish; working for others and learning about their lives often gives us new attitudes about ourselves.

- *Practice empathetic reactions*: Present a hypothetical problem situation a child might encounter (for example, a friend's parents have divorced or another friend's grandmother is dying). Discuss these questions together:

  ▶ What's the bad thing that happened?

  ▶ How is this person feeling about what happened?

  ▶ What can I do in response?

- *Praise positive behavior*: Catch kids doing good and reinforce that behavior, instead of harping on the negatives.

- *Provide opportunities for fellowship and friendship*: Parties, celebrations, projects, eating together, pen-pal relationships, and other such relational activities are warm and nurturing antidotes to negatives, and may fill up the holes in both a bully's and a target's life.

D Appendix

Sexual Harassment and Nonprofit Organizations

Sexual harassment in nonprofit organizations usually occurs as quid pro quo harassment or as hostile environment harassment. You'll want to be informed of and guard against both kinds in your church or nonprofit environment.

Quid Pro Quo Harassment

Quid pro quo harassment is defined as a person submitting to unwelcome sexual conduct either as a condition of becoming employed (unwelcome sexual conduct in exchange for an employment offer) or as a condition of maintaining employment or avoiding dismissal (unwelcome sexual conduct in exchange for promotions, higher compensation, positive evaluations, and so on).

Hostile Environment Harassment

Hostile environment harassment is defined as unwelcome sexual conduct by a supervisor, person in authority, or a peer this is so severe, persistent, or pervasive that it a) affects an individual's conduct or behavior; or b) affects a youth's ability to participate in or benefit from an activity; or c) creates an intimidating, threatening, or harmful environment.

Both kinds of harassment can affect staff and volunteers as well as youth who attend programs sponsored by a church or nonprofit organization. Staff, volunteers, or peers can harass children or youth. All too often, it's a group of peers who harass a child or teen; however, when an adult staff person or volunteer is subject to harassment by another person, it's usually by someone in authority over that person rather than by a group of the person's peers.

Examples of Sexual Harassment

- Touching of a sexual nature including prolonged hugging or kissing.
- Displaying or distributing sexually explicit drawings, pictures, and written materials including obscene materials and pornography.
- Use of the computer or online activities to create sexual material or display sexually explicit material.

- Sexual gestures, dirty jokes, offensive jokes, gender and racial slurs.
- Unwelcome flirtations, advances, propositions.
- Persistent and severe teasing and gossiping about sexual development, sexual behavior, or sexual orientation.
- Graphic or degrading comments about appearance, body development, or anatomy.
- Pressure for sexual favors, sexual contact, or sexual talk, such as sexual behavior, sexual interests, sexual fantasies.
- Stalking another person to pursue an unwelcome relationship.
- Verbal threats or forced attempts at unwelcome sexual conduct.

Suggestions for Preventing Sexual Harassment

- Establish guidelines for conduct in relationships among minors, among adults, and among adults and children or youth.
- Establish a policy identifying sexual harassment, how to report it, and how to respond to reports within the organization, applying state or provincial law when applicable.
- Conduct training about sexual harassment for staff, volunteers, and youth.
- Inform staff and volunteers about sexual harassment, how to prevent it, and how to respond to it.

Responding to Sexual Harassment

For the person being harassed

- Take sexual harassment seriously.
- If you can, tell the person the harassment must stop immediately.
- If it continues, seek out an adult or supervisor and inform him or her of the harassment.
- If fearful of or unable to talk to the harasser, seek out an adult or supervisor for assistance.
- Document all efforts to get the harasser to stop; collect any evidence to support the allegations, such as email or text messages, notes or letters, voicemail messages, gifts, photos, and so on.
- Tell someone and continue to update this person on events that may indicate the harassment is continuing.
- Ask someone to observe the interactions between the harasser and the person being harassed.

For the organization receiving a complaint against a staff person/ volunteer

- Take complaints of sexual harassment seriously.
- Seek legal consultation and input from experts as needed.

- The supervisor should inform the alleged harasser of the complaint and offer an opportunity to confront the allegations.
- If the alleged harasser either admits or does not deny the allegations, the supervisor needs to take action to reduce the threat of continuing harassment. Those actions may include

  ▶ supervising the contact between harasser and harassed.

  ▶ prohibiting contact between the harasser and the harassed.

  ▶ placing a written reprimand in the employee or volunteer's file.

  ▶ suspending the harasser or refusing to allow the harasser to attend organization-sponsored programs until the behavior ceases.

- If harassment continues, consider additional discipline including suspension (with pay) and in some cases termination. If the harasser is a volunteer or peer, discipline should include removal or dismissal from the position or barring the person from attending organization-sponsored activities.
- If a restraining order or peace order is necessary to prevent further contact with the person who has been harassed, the organization should support such action and should enforce restraining orders issued by the court.
- Parents of minors will be informed whenever a minor is accused of harassment or is the victim of harassment.

Issues to Consider When Investigating Complaints of Harassment

- **The severity of the conduct:** It's important to intervene when the harassment is persistent and pervasive. In addition, intervention is needed when verbal or non-verbal threats have been made to the alleged victim, since such threats could jeopardize that person's employment, safety, or emotional well-being. Level of severity is a subjective standard—it's always difficult to judge the impact of the harassment on the alleged victim.
- **The role or position of the harasser:** When the harasser is in a position of power or authority over the alleged victim, the organization's responsibility to intervene becomes greater. State or provincial law *requires* intervention in some circumstances; the organization faces a greater risk of liability if it fails to intervene.
- **The pattern of behavior:** An organization should not ignore a situation in which the reported harassment increases in frequency, increases in severity, or includes more than one victim. A pattern of engaging others through harassing behaviors requires the organization to intervene.

Resources
U.S. Federal Law: Title IX of the Education Amendments of 1972
Federal Register, Vol 62, No. 49, pages 12034-12051
Canadian Federal Law: Human Rights Act
Provincial Law: Provincial Human Rights Code and Provincial Human
Rights Commission

E Appendix

Guidelines for Reducing the Risk of Abuse in Friendship Ministries Programs

Introduction

Friendship Ministries was created for youth and adults with intellectual disabilities to help them draw closer to God. The success of Friendship groups depends on numerous dedicated volunteers and mentors who help persons with an intellectual disability develop a fuller understanding of God's love and grace.

The design of the program places people in one-to-one interpersonal relationships. Unfortunately, it is in the context of interpersonal relationships that persons with intellectual disabilities are often abused. Because of the potential risk of abuse, Friendship Ministries established the following guidelines. The organization recommends each Friendship group follow these guidelines so that Friendship meetings and social events will be enjoyable and safe for everyone.

Definitions
- *Friend* is a person participating in the Friendship group.
- *Volunteer/Mentor* is a person serving in the Friendship group.
- *Abuse* is harm or threatened harm to a friend committed by another person with real or apparent authority. There are several types of abuse:

  ▶ **Sexual abuse** is actual or threatened sexual exploitation of a friend including but not limited to sexual intimacy. It is considered sexual abuse if it meets the definition and the abuser is a caregiver or supervisor or maintains authority over the other person.

  ▶ **Physical abuse** is non-accidental physical injury, harm, or threatened harm to a friend who is under the care, supervision, or real/apparent authority of the person causing the physical injury or harm.

  ▶ **Emotional abuse** is the use of words, silence, or non-verbal behavior to threaten, intimidate, belittle, or humiliate a friend or to improperly influence or control their thoughts, feelings, or behaviors. Emotional abuse is usually chronic and severe, and results in the person being helpless, dependent on the abuser, and having low self-esteem.

▶ **Economic abuse** is the misuse or misappropriation of a friend's financial resources.

▶ **Spiritual abuse** is the misuse of Scripture, church doctrine or practice, or spiritual authority to improperly influence or control the thoughts, feelings, and behaviors of a friend. An example of spiritual abuse is forcing a friend to participate in an altar call.

General Guidelines

For all Friendship groups, Friendship Ministries recommends the following guidelines:

Group Meetings

- If a friend and mentor meet alone in a classroom, keep the classroom room door open.
- If possible, have pairs of mentors/friends meet in adjacent rooms.
- If the meeting room is large enough, then more than one mentor/friend pair could meet at the same time.
- Assign a volunteer to monitor the rooms where mentor/friend pairs are meeting.
- If the classroom doors need to remain closed, each door should have a window with an unobstructed view of the room.

Bathroom Guidelines

- When assistance is unexpected, friends should be assisted by someone of the same gender.
- When friends routinely need bathroom assistance or need assistance with medical devices, caregivers should provide this assistance. Make plans to assist the friend before attending the Friendship group.

Physical and Verbal Contact

- Physical affection initiated by a volunteer or mentor should be limited to side-to-side hugs, pats on the back or forearm, touching the back of the hand, and gently squeezing the hand.

- Both the friend and the volunteer/mentor can say no to physical affection and refrain from displays of affection. If a friend is unable to verbalize no, notice carefully their body language and facial expression that may indicate discomfort with physical affection.

- It isn't appropriate to make lewd or suggestive comments to friends or tell them dirty or off-color jokes. Details or discussions about one's intimate life shouldn't come up in a Friendship meeting.

Corrective Action

Consequences or corrections to attitude or behavior are sometimes necessary in a Friendship meeting. When consequences or corrections are needed, these guidelines may help, but they are not progressive steps of consequence or correction.

- Give a verbal reminder to follow the rules.
- Involve another mentor, volunteer, guardian, or caregiver.
- Ask the friend to leave the room for a few minutes and take a timeout.
- End the meeting.
- Ask the friend not to come to the program for a period of time until an agreement can be reached about acceptable behavior.
- If a situation arises away from the Friendship program, stay in a public setting because moving to a private or isolated setting may increase vulnerability for the mentor and the friend. Use a cell phone to seek assistance or to relay to someone else what is happening.
- If problems continue beyond minor correction, do not hesitate to involve a parent, guardian, or caregiver and inform them how the situation was handled.

Physical intervention by a mentor or volunteer including slapping, hitting, kicking, or punching is never appropriate. Physical restraint by a mentor or volunteer may be necessary, but only to prevent harm or injury to the friend, mentor, or other people nearby. Lashing out in anger or a verbal attack by a mentor or volunteer will likely cause more harm to a friend and to the relationship.

Off-Site or Home Visits

What a blessing it can be when friends and mentors enjoy a friendship apart from the group meeting. Friendship Ministries recommends the following guidelines:

- Mentors should learn about the friend's interests and pursue those with him or her.
- Mentors and friends should encourage one another to discover spiritual gifts and use them outside the Friendship program.
- Mentors should involve their family members in activities with a friend to increase socialization and interaction.
- Mentors should check with a friend's parent, guardian, or caregiver before making plans to socialize. Be sure to leave a phone number and the location where the mentor and friend will be. Inform a parent,

guardian, or caregiver when the mentor will pick up and drop off the friend.

- When a friend comes to visit, a mentor's family should not entertain him or her. If the mentor's schedule does not permit a visit, reschedule the visit.
- If the friend is living independently, leave a note explaining where the friend is and with whom.

Transportation

Friendship Ministries recommends the following guidelines:

- Mentors who transport friends must have a valid driver's license and insurance coverage on the vehicle and passengers.
- Mentors should make sure there are seatbelts for each passenger.
- Mentors should carry a cell phone in case of medical emergency, accident or injury, vehicle breakdown, weather-related problems, and to keep people informed of pick-ups and drop-offs.
- Mentors may have another adult in the vehicle so that one may drive and one may interact with the friend.

Supervision

Adequate supervision is important before and after Friendship group meetings. Friendship Ministries recommends the following guidelines:

- Before and after Friendship group meets, a suggested ratio is one volunteer or mentor to three friends.
- During study sessions, a one-to-one ratio is preferred.
- For off-site activities, a one-to-one ratio is preferred, depending on the activity and the location. (Before and after Friendship group meets, guardians and caregivers may be included in the ratio if they are supervising the friends.)

Screening

Friendship Ministries and friend's parents, guardians, and caregivers want suitable volunteers and mentors to study with and socialize with friends. If the Friendship group has more than two volunteers or mentors or if the group is looking to recruit volunteers or mentors, Friendship Ministries recommends the following guidelines:

- Existing groups larger than two volunteers or mentors should initiate screening steps including an application, reference checks, and interview.
- Groups recruiting new volunteers or mentors should initiate screening steps including an application, reference checks, and interview.

- An applicant can be denied a volunteer or mentor position for any reason.
- Information about applicants should be stored in a private manner. If possible, store application materials in a locked cabinet.
- Volunteers or mentors who receive information about an applicant that indicates previous misconduct or inappropriate behavior should deny the applicant a position for the best interest of the Friendship group.

Reporting

If a volunteer or mentor becomes aware of a possible or actual abuse situation, take action to protect a friend. Friendship Ministries recommends the following guidelines:

- By state law, some volunteers and mentors are mandatory reporters who are required to report a suspicion of abuse against a minor or vulnerable adult. Friendship groups should support mandatory reporters when they need to report a suspicion of abuse.
- In Canada, everyone is legally responsible to report a suspicion of abuse against a minor or vulnerable adult. Friendship groups should support those legally required to report.
- For all others who serve in Friendship groups, Friendship groups should encourage them to consider it their moral and ethical duty to report a suspicion of abuse.

Although reporting suspected abuse is unsettling, friends rely on volunteers and mentors who become aware of abuse and inappropriate behavior to take action to correct it. Because direct intervention could put both the alleged victim and the volunteer or mentor at risk, volunteers and mentors should seek out local resources and civil authorities trained and qualified to intervene.

When the friend is a minor (under the age of eighteen in most states and provinces), contact Children's Protective Services or Children's Aid Society. When the friend is an adult (eighteen years of age and older in most states and provinces), Adult Protective Services should be contacted.

The person who witnesses abuse or hears directly from a friend about possible abuse is the *firsthand reporter*. This firsthand reporter usually has anonymity when he or she reports to civil authorities.

Because abuse can include violent behavior and the abuser can be unpredictable, volunteers and mentors should refrain from intervening with anyone accused of abuse—except in an emergency to stop an abusive incident in their presence.

If a volunteer or mentor shows signs of abusive behavior or repeatedly demonstrates behaviors that are unacceptable towards friends, a group leader or other volunteers and mentors should ask that person to withdraw from the ministry. Furthermore, if a volunteer or mentor is asked to provide a reference for someone they witnessed or were suspicious of engaging in inappropriate behavior, the wisest and safest thing to do would be to not recommend that person.

Allegations of spiritual abuse are not forwarded to civil authorities; those matters should be referred to church officials for follow-up.

Retention/Response:
Friendship Ministries recommends the following guidelines for alleged offenders:
- If a volunteer or mentor confesses to or is found guilty of abuse, he or she should be removed from the Friendship group. If the matter was not reported to civil authorities, it should also be done.
- If a volunteer or mentor is accused of abuse, a replacement should be sought until the allegations are either substantiated or discharged. If the allegations are unfounded, the formerly accused may be allowed back into the Friendship group. However, if the allegations are substantiated, the accused should be removed.
- Friendship groups can protect friends and volunteers or mentors by not approving someone to serve who has confessed or been found guilty of harming a minor or vulnerable adult. The risk of re-offending is high.

Friendship Ministries recommends the following guidelines for alleged victims:
- A friend abused or allegedly abused should be helped to find an appropriate counselor trained in abuse dynamics and services to intellectually disabled persons.
- A friend abused or allegedly abused should be encouraged to cooperate with an investigation by civil authorities.

This document was prepared jointly by the office of Abuse Prevention and staff of Friendship Ministries, April 2004.

F Appendix
Facility Walking Tour Checklist

At-Risk Locations
Which of these locations are found in your facility?
- Infant or Toddler Rooms: _____ yes _____ no
- Preschool Children Rooms: _____ yes _____ no
- School-Age Children Classrooms: _____ yes _____ no
- Multi-Purpose Classrooms: _____ yes _____ no
- Recreation Room or Gymnasium: _____ yes _____ no
- Teen Club or Meeting Rooms: _____ yes _____ no
- Boys and Girls Club Meeting Rooms: _____ yes _____ no
- Bathrooms: _____ yes _____ no
- Locked Closets, Maintenance Rooms: _____ yes _____ no
- Staff or Volunteer offices: _____ yes _____ no
- Library or Resource Room: _____ yes _____ no
- Bus or Van: _____ yes _____ no
- Kitchen: _____ yes _____ no
- Workshop or Craft Room: _____ yes _____ no
- Other Room or Facility Use: _____ yes _____ no
- Off-Site Facility: _____ yes _____ no

Questions to Ask about the Facility and Rooms
- Is there an unobstructed view of the entire room?
- Is there a bathroom within the infant or toddler area?
- Is a bathroom located near the rooms used by the youngest children?
- Which rooms are locked? Who has a key or card to locked rooms?
- Can children use door handles easily?
- Are nursery and classrooms located near each other?
- Is a classroom or program activity isolated from the other rooms or activities?

- Are program activities routinely held away from the facility?
- Is visual inspection into rooms and offices possible?
- Does the arrangement of furniture allow visual inspection of activities?
- Is the volunteer or staff visible from the door or window?

What policies might make these places safer?

At-Risk Situations
Which of these situations apply to your organization?
- Permit one-to-one meetings with minors: ____ yes ____ no
- Permit frequent and lengthy meetings with minors: ____ yes ____ no
- Permit counseling sessions with minors: ____ yes ____ no
- Meetings take place in isolated places or off-site: ____ yes ____ no
- Discipline of minors is permitted: ____ yes ____ no
- Volunteers and staff meet with youth unsupervised: ____ yes ____ no
- Some staff or volunteers are untrained or inexperienced: ____ yes ____ no
- Program participants include minors who are walk-ins, friends of attending youth, or unknown to staff and volunteers: ____ yes ____ no

Questions about Supervision:
- How many volunteers are assigned to each room or program meeting?
- What is the minimum age of volunteers in each room or program meeting?
- Are staff and volunteers screened?
- Are staff and volunteers supervised?
- What supervision and accountability tools are used?
- Are staff and volunteers trained for their positions?
- Are behavioral guidelines posted for volunteers, staff, and youth?

What policies or procedures might reduce the risk of these situations?

See Appendix G, "Facility Changes for the Protection of Youth," for suggestions for making your facility a safer place for children and youth.

G Appendix

Facility Changes for the Protection of Youth

After taking a walking tour of your facility and assessing whether it's a safe place for children and youth, you may want to think about making some changes to ensure greater safety. Here are some good ideas to consider:

Bathrooms

- Bathrooms with two or three stalls are safer than single-stall bathrooms because of the possibility of leaving the door slightly ajar while still maintaining privacy.
- Classrooms or activity rooms for the youngest children in your programs should be closest to bathroom facilities.
- A single commode bathroom within a nursery is advisable so that volunteers don't need to take children out for toileting. The door of a bathroom located in the nursery should be fitted so that the top half swings open. Toileting can be supervised with the upper part open; privacy can be maintained by closing the top.
- Place changing tables for infants *inside* the nursery room. This makes supervision simple and requests for assistance easily met.
- Fit multiple-stall bathrooms located near the nursery with a bar that prevents the door from closing completely or use a rubber stop to keep the door slightly ajar.
- Always observe local fire and safety codes—the bathroom door located on a fire-rated corridor may or may not be propped open depending on the code in that location.

Classrooms

- Fit all classroom doors with a safety-glass insert so that the activity inside the room can be monitored without disrupting the class. The lower edge of the glass should be even with the door handle. The glass insert should not be covered with a curtain when minors are using the room. Note: This is true even when audio/visual equipment is being used and room darkening is preferred.

- When safety-glass inserts are used, a complete view of the room is not always possible. In that case, place concave mirrors in a corner of the room to allow for a more complete view.
- Design new classrooms so that the teacher is fully visible through the safety-glass insert. Also, make sure storage units do not obstruct the view of the room through the glass insert. Make sure storage areas don't create pockets or crannies that hide activities or people.
- Do not fit classrooms with locks unless security is a concern. In that case, classrooms should be locked when not in use.
- Fit locked classrooms with lever handles and a lock set that allows young children to manipulate the lock and the door handle.
- Group classrooms together (a classroom off by itself should be monitored). Follow local fire and safety codes that specify whether classroom doors should swing out and whether room capacity requires one door or two.

Nursery

- Install a safety-glass insert in the nursery room door, as well as a concave mirror if necessary.
- Install a roll-up window between the counter top and the bulkhead or ceiling.
- Place a two-way mirror in the nursery so that parents can observe the children without the children knowing the parents are there.
- A door with a swing-top makes handy access for parents and attendants. Leave the bottom half closed for the protection of the children inside the room while opening the top half so that parents can drop off children and pick them up.
- When more than one nursery room is needed, it is ideal to locate them next to each other so facilities can be shared. Install a two-way mirror or a glass window between the two rooms. Similarly, set up a walkie-talkie or intercom system to assist attendants in the case of a crisis.
- Periodically clean all toys, games, and equipment and check them for safety.
- Stock a first aid kit in the nursery room, post basic first aid tips, and make first aid training available for all volunteers and staff working with youth.
- Set up a telephone or paging system so that volunteers can call for emergency assistance.

Staff and Volunteer Offices

- Fit office doors with a safety-glass insert. (Make sure the view through the insert is not obstructed.)

- Place the furniture in the office so that the staff or volunteer faces the door. The staff or volunteer should be visible at all times through the insert.
- Fit offices with chairs rather than couches.
- If the organization has several offices, group them together. Offices should not have an egress to the outside; exiting to a common area is preferred. Offices should not be located in the basement or down isolated corridors.

Storage Closets and Maintenance Rooms

- Keep closet doors and doors into maintenance rooms locked when church programs are in session.
- Fit doors with a lock set that allows young children to manipulate the lock and the door handle from within.
- If building regulations permit, fit the doors with a safety-glass insert.
- Convert to swipe cards to unlock these rooms. Swipe cards are easier to track and harder to copy. (Keep a list of those who have swipe cards.)

Exits

- Limit the number of open access points to the building during program hours. Limit access from the outside to doors that are closest to the classrooms or where the youngest children meet.
- Fit doors to the outside with bar locks that allow for easy opening from the inside while locked to outside traffic.
- Lock exits near restrooms and classrooms during program times. These exits also should be fitted with a bar lock for easy egress.
- Exits that are not primarily used for access to or egress from the building should remain locked at all times and fitted with a bar lock for ease of exiting from within—especially if the door is used as a fire exit or in case of emergencies.

In addition to fire and safety codes and building regulations, nonprofit organizations must also follow state or provincial statutes that govern the use of facilities by persons with disabilities.

For more helpful information, visit these websites:

- Americans with Disabilities Act—www.usdoj.gov/crt/ada/
- Canadian Charter of Rights and Freedoms—http://laws.justice.gc.ca/en/charter
- Human Resources and Social Development Canada Office for Disability Issues—www.hrsdc.gc.ca/en/disability_issues/mandate/index.shtml

Thanks to Calvin Jen for his contribution to these guidelines. Cal is an Associate Professor of Business at Calvin College and the founder of AMDG Architects, Grand Rapids, Michigan.

H Appendix
Sample Incident Report Form

Name of person making the report: _____

Date of report:_____Phone number: _____

Volunteer/staff position: _____

Description of the circumstances (when incident occurred/was reported, location, time of day, persons present at the time)

Description of the incident (reported or witnessed)
Who:

What:

When:

Where:

Names of any witnesses_____

_____

If a reasonable suspicion of child abuse exists, when was Children's Protective Services or the Police Department notified?_____

Caller's name_____

Caller's signature_____

Other action taken, if any _____

_____

Date Child Safety Committee received report_____

I Appendix

Responding to a Child's Report of Abuse

When a child reports something to you that raises suspicion the child may have witnessed or been a victim of abuse, these guidelines for responding may be helpful to you:

- Take the child's story seriously.

- Don't respond with judgmental statements such as, "I think you just had a bad dream."

- Don't react with fear or disgust at the child's story; that may cause the child to stop talking or to think you are upset with him or her.

- Don't try to convince the child that the story isn't true or that it did not happen the way the child is reporting it.

- Don't promise the child that you will not tell anyone what he or she shared with you.

- Remind the child that whatever happened was not his or her fault.

- Remind the child that it was a good decision to tell you what happened to him or her.

- Tell the child that you want to find help to prevent another incident from happening.

- Don't offer the child a reward for telling the story or promise the child a gift if he or she tells another adult.

- Reassure the child that he or she does not deserve to be hurt by anyone.

- Don't frighten the child by talking about police involvement or medical examinations to verify the complaint; instead, share with the child that other people need to know about what happened, and they will talk to the child later.

- Don't ask the child to show you any bruises that are beneath his or her clothing or underwear; simply note those bruises that are not concealed. In some communities, removing a child's clothing even to confirm a report of abuse is a violation of the law.

- Don't investigate the child's story; rather, listen to the story and take notes immediately afterwards while the story is still fresh in your mind.

- Don't tell the child that he or she was abused.

- Offer support to the child and remind the child that you care about him or her.

- Follow up during the next weeks and months by speaking to the child and offering support.

J

Appendix

Suggested Media Disclosure Policy

Every organization that deals with abuse faces the dilemma of disclosure. On the one hand, alleged victims and their families may feel embarrassment, be subject to requests for information, or worse yet, face isolation and rejection. The alleged offender and his or her family risk harm to reputation before the alleged events are dismissed or proven, whether in a court of law or through dissemination of information within the organization.

On the other hand, if the organization does not disclose an alleged incident of abuse, the organization can't assist either the party harmed or the accused. The organization will be unable to safeguard other youth in similar situations. And, furthermore, it can be held liable if further abuse happens.

Some basic guidelines are needed to (a) protect victims from further abuse, (b) protect accused persons from unfair prejudice, (c) prevent additional persons from being victimized, (d) allow the legal process to take its course, (e) promote healing, and (f) permit treatment to begin. Here are some guidelines that may help:

Timing Is Critical

Releasing information lets the alleged victim know that he or she is believed. It also informs the alleged perpetrator that acts of misconduct will not be kept secret. Disclosure lets a congregation or community know that abuse allegedly occurred, and it also encourages the organization and the parties to strive for prevention, healing, and forgiveness.

The disclosure itself must include only facts—not suspicion or innuendo. This doesn't mean that an investigation is complete; it simply means disclosing the nature of the abuse, the name of the alleged abuser, and when the abuse allegedly happened. Disclosure should not be made before the alleged offender is confronted by civil authorities, but it should be made as soon as possible to prevent further abuse. Both the alleged victim(s) and the alleged offender ought to be advised that a disclosure will be made.

Who Should Disclose?

Disclosure should be made by a person in the organization with a minimal relationship to either the alleged victim or the alleged offender. The designated individual should present only the facts of the matter and should avoid interpreting, minimizing, rationalizing, or making suggestions about how to resolve the situation.

Don't Minimize the Situation

The disclosure should not minimize the abuse that has taken place, nor the alleged victim's response to the abuse. The person making the disclosure should acknowledge that it's painful for everyone involved in the situation.

Distribute a Written Statement

A written statement should be distributed at the time of disclosure. Also, if possible, the speaker can suggest written resources and websites about abuse to educate and create awareness.

Form a Team

The disclosure ought to include the announcement that a team will be formed to help both the alleged victim and the alleged offender through the legal and organizational process as well as the process of healing and forgiveness.

Develop a Plan to Deal with the Incident

The disclosure should include a plan for what the organization will do as a result of this alleged abuse incident. Subsequent disclosures should keep the community or congregation informed of the steps taken, how the plan might change, and any results from the steps taken thus far.

Confidentiality versus Secrecy

The disclosure will always involve weighing the matter of confidentiality versus secrecy. Confidentiality or privileged communication is not an appropriate defense for protecting a perpetrator or failing to alert vulnerable members of the congregation or community.

The alleged abuser's name should be disclosed if
- the person has a position of leadership in the organization or church.

- the person has been asked to step aside from any position of leadership in the organization or church.

- the person would have contact with youth or other vulnerable members of the organization, church or community.

- the person has been arrested or charged with a crime against youth.

- the person makes threats against the alleged victim.

- the person continues to contact the alleged victim or attempts to harm him or her again.

The alleged victim's name should not be disclosed. In addition, if the alleged victim might be identifiable as part of a group, then the group should not be named either. For example, if the alleged victim plays on an eight-member basketball team, no mention should be made of the team. In addition, the alleged victim's name should not be disclosed if the alleged offender is a relative of the alleged victim.

K Appendix

Sample Letter to the Congregation

Dear Brothers and Sisters in Christ,

It is with very heavy hearts that we write this letter to you.

A youth (unnamed) from our congregation (or community)
recently came forward with an allegation of misconduct against
_____ (name of alleged abuser). The
alleged misconduct occurred when the youth was attending a church-
sponsored event.

We cannot identify the specific misconduct, but civil authorities
were notified of the allegation, and they have begun an investigation.
The investigation may take several weeks. Until the investigation
concludes, the governing body has decided to suspend (or remove)
_____ from positions of caregiving,
supervision, or authority.

Over the past several days, we have prayerfully sought wisdom and
direction. We've consulted with denominational, civil, and legal
authorities. We've carefully sought out advice so that we might respond
to this matter pastorally and justly. We have convened a special (board/
council) meeting to pray and to consider what we should do.

We encourage you to pray for this youth and the family. We encourage
you to pray for _____ (name of alleged abuser)
and the family.

We realize that this situation will raise many questions in your minds. If
you have questions or need to talk to someone, we invite you to contact
the pastor or a (board/council) member. If you have reason to believe
that _____ had inappropriate contact with another
youth or member of this congregation, we also ask you to contact the
pastor or a board member.

Our intent from this point on is to cooperate with the investigation and to provide pastoral care for the youth, for _____, for their respective families, and to this congregation.

We acknowledge that this is a painful event in the life of our congregation. The (board/council) is working on a plan to begin the healing and restoration process. If we persevere in love for others, and if we seek justice for the wronged, we will grow from this sad event into the safe haven we long to provide for our children and youth.

(Name),
On behalf of (name of the governing body of the church)

L

Appendix

Sample Letter to the Community

Dear Friends and Supporters,

We need to inform you of a serious matter that recently came to our attention.

A youth (unnamed) came forward with an allegation of misconduct against _____ (name of person), a volunteer (or staff person) with _____ (name of organization). The alleged misconduct occurred when the youth was attending an event (or program) sponsored by _____ _____ (name of organization).

We cannot identify the specific conduct, but the allegation was reported to the civil authorities, who have begun an investigation. The investigation may take several weeks. Until the investigation concludes, the Board of Directors has decided to suspend (or remove) _____ from any responsibilities with youth.

We have consulted with civil, legal, and other authorities for advice so that we can respond to this matter swiftly, cautiously, and justly. While we desire to be open and forthcoming about this matter, there are reasonable limitations placed on us to preserve the integrity of the investigation and the privacy of the parties.

We realize that this situation will raise many questions in your minds. If you have a specific question about the care of youth in our programs, please contact the executive director or board chairperson whose names appear below.

Our focus is to cooperate with the investigation, maintain support to the parties, and provide quality care for the youth in our programs. We are reviewing all safety procedures, which is customary when allegations of misconduct occur. We assure you that we have made every reasonable effort to protect the youth in our programs and we will continue to do so.

We ask for your continued support of the staff and volunteers who work diligently to serve youth with quality programs. We also ask for your patience as this important investigation continues. We will inform you of more details as we are able to do so.

(Name), Executive Director   (Name), Chair of the Board
(name of organization)   (name of organization)

M Appendix
Signs and Symptoms of Child Abuse

Recognizing signs and symptoms of abuse is not a simple matter. Children rarely exhibit just one sign that suggests they have been the victims of abuse. And some symptoms may also represent typical developmental changes or the aftereffects of traumas other than abuse in a child's life. Conversely, it's possible for abuse to be taking place without the *appearance* of noticeable symptoms because children have the ability to mask or deny something in their lives that would otherwise be very confusing and painful to acknowledge. Generally, when you observe several signs over a period of time, it may suggest that a child is suffering from abuse. The complexity of this process of observation highlights the need for training among volunteers, staff, and program leaders. Here are some typical signs and symptoms that may alert you to be attentive to the possibility of abuse or neglect:

Infants and Preschool Children
- Regression to an earlier stage of behavioral development such as baby talk, thumb sucking, or bedwetting
- Change in social behavior—excessive crying or clinging, becoming aggressive or withdrawn—that is not associated with normal developmental stages
- Physical manifestations such as loss of bowel control, bedwetting, frequent urination, headaches, stomachaches, breathing difficulties, sore throats accompanied by gagging, stains in the child's underclothes
- Exhibiting signs of fear around a family member or a familiar person; fear of a familiar place or object
- Fear of being touched, shying away from physical contact; resistance to being diapered or assisted in the bathroom
- Use of explicit language or sexual behavior that is beyond the child's comprehension or life experience
- Attempting sexual behavior with other children or attending adults
- Unexplained injuries and/or bruises, repeated injuries blamed on the child's carelessness, multiple bruises sustained in one event, or bruises to child's midsection, back, head, or back of thighs; signs of scalding,

burning, or distinctive bruising, such as in the shape of a belt buckle; multiple bruises in various stages of healing

- Name-calling or bullying behavior toward other children, sulking or brooding
- Fascination with fire, playing with matches and lighters

School-Age Children

- Physical manifestations as above, with addition of complaints of pain, irritation, soreness, redness on the child's bottom
- Smearing feces on walls or objects
- Pattern of injuries, multiple injuries, injuries about the face or neck; failure to complain about or explain an obvious physical discomfort
- Unusual fears—a familiar person, a particular room, a particular object, or fear of new experiences
- Poor concentration in classroom
- Exhibiting adult-pleasing behaviors, striving for perfection, acting miserable if failing
- Engaging in self-injury; engaging in excessive masturbation or masturbation in public setting
- Acting enraged and out of control; expressing anger through destruction
- Shyness about physical touch
- Exhibiting sexual behavior beyond comprehension or maturity level; behaving in a sexual manner with other children or adults
- Exhibiting signs of needing to be in control of others or situations, bullying others
- Hostility and distrust of adults, mood swings and irritability, violent disruptions
- Acting out, including hoarding food and toys, lying, stealing, assaulting
- Frequent absences from school or other scheduled events either because of being punished or to hide bruises
- Low self-esteem, particular sensitivity to criticism
- Hyper-vigilance—excessive and suspicious watching of other people; easily startled
- Preoccupation with fire and setting fires

Adolescents

- Eating disorders, use of laxatives, unexplained and dramatic changes in weight
- Change in sleep patterns, including excessive sleeping, sleeping during the day, and insomnia
- Plunge in school performance

- Perfectionist behavior, excessive self-criticism, attempting to please adults, overreacting to any form of criticism or complaint
- Sexually provocative or asexual behavior, denial of body changes and sexual development; for females, seeking affection from older adult males
- Experimentation with drugs and alcohol
- Self-abusive behavior including cutting self, preoccupation with danger and weapons, suicide attempts
- Truancy from school
- Cruelty to animals, bullying younger children
- Emotional numbness, inability to be emotionally supportive to others
- Having few friends, changing friends often
- Depression and other signs of withdrawal and avoidance
- Pregnancy
- Refusing to attend to basic hygiene
- Rectal and vaginal infections
- Hyper-vigilance—excessive and suspicious watching of other people; easily startled

Signs of Neglect
- Appearing to be underfed, constantly hungry, underweight for size and age
- Begging for food, stealing food, hoarding food
- Lack of supervision, underage child supervising another child/other children
- Chronic absenteeism from school, unattended educational needs
- Unattended medical, dental needs
- Consistent or frequent lack of hygiene, poor hygiene, or lack of cleanliness resulting in odors
- For infants, failure to thrive

Parental Behaviors and Home Life
- Not attending meetings about the child, not showing an interest in the child, critical of child, uncomplimentary
- Constantly putting child down, using harsh words to describe child, using threats and unflattering language
- Describing child as underachiever, complaining that he/she lets people down, is unmotivated, achieves less than brothers and sisters
- Speaking of child in way that sounds romantic, too grown-up, too sugary, too perfect
- Hostile, closed-minded, overprotective, isolating, doesn't let others in the house, won't participate in activities with other parents, makes excuses about failing to do tasks, talks about things not being good at home

- Reports of past/other suspicious behavior, reports that an older brother or sister may have been mistreated
- Chemical dependency by one or both parents
- Sudden and dramatic changes in family's financial security

N Appendix

Code of Ethics for Volunteers and Staff in Child and Youth Programs (in Churches)

Believing that God is calling me to serve children or youth in this congregation,

- My first priority in supervising or volunteering with children or youth will be to seek their spiritual, psychological, and social welfare.
- I will respect each child or youth's cultural and ethnic background.
- I will give the parent(s) of each child or youth full information about the program I am supervising or volunteering in.
- I will not intentionally harm or betray a child or youth's trust. I will use reasonable means to protect each child or youth from abuse while he or she is in my care.
- I will report a reasonable suspicion of abuse of a child or youth to a responsible person for a proper investigation.
- If I wish to talk to a child or youth alone, it will be within the sight and sound of one or more adults.
- I will answer a child or youth's questions openly and honestly.
- I will work with the children or youth to set guidelines for acceptable behavior within the group. I will expect children or youth to act based on those guidelines. If a child or youth consistently breaks behavioral guidelines, I will seek help from parents and others to assist me in responding.
- If a child or youth is distressed, I will try to offer comfort and help, and I will encourage the child or youth to find appropriate help.
- I will pray for each child or youth regularly and assure them that I care about them.
- I will follow the policies and procedures in the congregation's Child Safety Policy.

_____   _____
Signature   Date

_____   _____
Volunteer or Staff Position   Supervisor's name

Appendix

Code of Ethics for Volunteers and Staff in Child and Youth Programs (in Nonprofit Organizations)

- My priority in supervising or volunteering with children or youth will be to seek their physical and emotional well-being.
- I will respect each child or youth's cultural and ethnic background.
- I will give the parent(s) of each child or youth full information about the program I am supervising or volunteering in.
- I will not intentionally harm or betray a child or youth's trust. I will use reasonable means to protect each child or youth from abuse while he or she is in my care.
- I will report a reasonable suspicion of abuse of a child or youth to a responsible person for a proper investigation.
- If I wish to talk to a child or youth alone, it will be within the sight and sound of one or more adults.
- I will answer a child or youth's questions openly and honestly.
- I will work with the children or youth to set guidelines for acceptable behavior within the group. I will expect children or youth to act based on those guidelines. If a child or youth consistently breaks behavioral guidelines, I will seek help from parents and others to assist me in responding.
- If a child or youth is distressed, I will try to offer comfort and help. I will encourage the child or youth to find the appropriate helps.
- I will follow the policies and procedures in the organization's Child Safety Policy.

_____   _____
           Signature   Date

_____   _____
  Volunteer or Staff Position   Supervisor's name

P Appendix
Case Studies

Case Study #1
From The Gazette, *section B, page 1: "Church Worker Accused of Abuse"*

The pastor of the Bible Church confirmed late yesterday that the police have questioned a volunteer from the church. This followed allegations of child abuse by a parent earlier this month. Details are sketchy, but the pastor reports that the thirty-seven-year-old female volunteer has been a member of the church for the past two years. The pastor would not disclose the name of the volunteer but said the volunteer was very reliable and well-liked. "I always thought the person got along well with children," the pastor stated. "There were never any complaints before now. I'm baffled and really don't know what to make of this."

According to Inspector Jones from the police department, the volunteer spent one morning a week at the church, babysitting infants and toddlers while their mothers attended a Bible study in another part of the church. As many as seven youngsters were under the volunteer's care each week. Jones indicated that earlier this year, two mothers noticed suspicious bruises on their children and each mother met with a church official who remains unidentified. The official apparently suggested the mothers meet with the volunteer about the matter. It is unclear whether the mothers did this. Both women declined to be interviewed citing privacy reasons. Some time later, one of the mothers brought her child to a pediatrician, who notified police authorities. Inspector Jones declined to comment on the child's injuries, but said the child was treated and released from a local hospital and is doing well.

For discussion:
- List and talk about the issues this news story raises.
- Describe the dynamics of abuse that are present.
- Discuss what policies Bible Church might have put in place to prevent this incident.
- Evaluate the church official's suggestion to the mothers that they talk to the volunteer.
- If the volunteer is charged, what defense might she present?
- Because the child is too young to testify, how will charges be determined?
- What should be the church's response to the children and their families?
- What should be the church's response to the alleged offender?

For discussion:
- List and talk about the issues that this story raises.
- Describe the dynamics of abuse that are present.
- Discuss policies that Youth Pride might have put in place to prevent this incident.
- If Nikki reports the incident, what should Youth Pride's response be to Dennis?
- If Nikki accuses Dennis of wrongdoing, what will he likely say in his defense?
- How could Youth Pride be liable in this situation? What could prevent them from being liable?

Case Study #2
Nikki's story

Nikki is fifteen years old and attends Youth Pride, a program that sponsors youth activities designed to keep teens out of gangs and away from drugs. Nikki lives about five miles from the Youth Pride office, and she relies on volunteers to take her home after midweek meetings and activities. A couple of weeks ago, Nikki rode home with a volunteer named Dennis.

Youth Pride has a transportation policy that states that a Youth Pride attendee can sit in the front seat with a Youth Pride driver *only if* there are other volunteers or attendees in the vehicle. Though they were alone, Dennis insisted that Nikki sit in the front seat with him. He said it would look strange to have her in the back seat, as if he was her chauffeur. Nikki teased him about being a cute chauffeur, but she climbed in the front seat anyway because she wanted to go home.

At the Dairy Den on the way out of town, Dennis pulled in and said, "Want an ice cream?" Nikki wasn't hungry, but said okay to be polite. They sat in the van at the far edge of the parking lot. Dennis and Nikki talked about Youth Pride for a while. Then Dennis reached into the back seat. He asked Nikki if she'd like some magazines to take home and read. Thinking that she was being offered freebies of *Rolling Stone*, her eyes lit up and she nodded yes. Dennis pulled out a *Hustler* magazine and asked her to look through it with him. Nikki didn't object, so Dennis started flipping through the pages, making comments about the nude pictures and the sex scenes. He invited Nikki to comment, too. Although shy at first, she chimed in with a few comments of her own.

When she looked at the clock on the dashboard, she realized that over an hour had passed. Nikki said she had to go, but Dennis insisted they look at one more magazine. Nikki got upset and demanded Dennis take her home. Then Dennis got mad, called her a slut, and told her if she didn't change her attitude with him, he could turn the Youth Pride staff against her. Dennis dropped Nikki off at home nearly two hours after they had left the Youth Pride meeting.

Case Study #3
Paul's predicament

Paul's idea of a perfect Sunday morning was devouring the sports section of the paper in his bedroom—reading it word for word, front to back. Paul's nickname through high school was "Triv" because he knew trivia about every sport and its respective stars. Paul played on the high school soccer team that made the finals two years in a row. For a while, Paul dreamed of receiving an athletic scholarship to attend college. Then, in his senior year he blew out his knee on a gopher hole on the school's practice field.

He almost missed the article—it was short and tucked under an advertisement for the region's only bowling center. But in that small article was an announcement that the soccer coach for Sports World, Inc., had been arrested. There were allegations about improper conduct with his players—including charges of sodomy and molestation in hotel rooms while traveling to soccer tournaments.

Paul could feel his heart beating in his chest and felt his cheeks flush. His breath quickened as he sat dazed and thought about his coach. Rising from the back of his mind, a memory surfaced—a memory of a hotel room outside the capital city. Paul was there for the regional all-star game. He had kicked the winning goal, and Coach asked him to come to his room to congratulate him. Paul couldn't remember being happier—to have Coach's attention and praise all to him was a dream! But something happened in that room that night. Paul remembers leaving the room early in the morning, wearing his shorts and carrying his pants. He let himself into the room he was sharing with a teammate and slipped under the covers. Paul woke up a different person.

Paul's hands are shaking as he puts the newspaper down. He goes into the bathroom and showers until the water is cold and numbing. He'd like to wash it all away.

For discussion:
- List and discuss the issues that Paul's story raises.
- Describe the dynamics of abuse that are present.
- Discuss policies that Sports World, Inc., might have put in place to prevent this incident.
- What should Sports World, Inc., do if Paul calls to report the incident?
- Is Sports World, Inc., liable in Paul's case? What defense will Sports World use?
- What factors may lead Paul to report or *not* to report the incident?
- Because Paul is an adult now, what impact does his age have on reporting this incident?
- What, if any, are the consequences to Paul if he chooses not to report the incident?

Q Appendix

Sample Parental Consent and Medical Form

Organization Name_____

Organization Address_____

We/I_____
parent(s) or guardian(s)

give permission for _____
name of child

to attend activities (outings, group activities, work projects, campouts, and so on) sponsored by the organization on or off the organization's property.

Activity name (to be filled in by organization) _____

_____

_____

Activity supervisors (to be filled in by organization) _____

_____

_____

We/I give permission to the supervisors of the activity to secure needed emergency medical treatment for the child named above. In case of accident or injury during the activity, we/I release the supervisors from all liability not covered by insurance.

Parent/guardian signature _____

Date_____

Telephone/cell number_____

Family's insurance company _____

Policy number_____

Allergies _____

Current medications (name, dosage, time of administration) _____

_____

_____

Other pertinent medical information_____

_____

_____

This parental consent and medical form is valid until_____
                                                                    date

R Appendix

Sample Transportation Consent Form

I_____(parent/guardian) of

_____(child/minor), give permission for

_____(name of organization)

to transport my child/teenager/ward to:

Name of event_____

Date of event_____

Pick up time _____Drop off time_____

(Name of organization) confirms that _____

is the designated driver for this event.

This driver has full insurance coverage on his or her vehicle:
Yes____ No____

This driver's record has been reviewed for points:
Yes____ No____

I hereby give consent for my child/ward to be transported by a designated driver approved by _____ (organization). I waive the driver and the organization from liability due to accidental injury suffered in a motor vehicle accident while a passenger in the vehicle.

_____
Parent/Guardian Signature   Date

_____
Driver Signature   Date

S Appendix

National Child Protection Act of 1993

An Act

To establish procedures for national criminal background checks for child care providers. Be it enacted by the Senate and House of Representatives of the United States of America in Congress assembled.

SECTION 1: SHORT TITLE.

This Act may be cited as the "National Child Protection Act of 1993."

SECTION 2: REPORTING CHILD ABUSE CRIME INFORMATION.

A. IN GENERAL. In each State, an authorized criminal justice agency of the State shall report child abuse crime information to, or index child abuse crime information in, the national criminal history background check system.

B. PROVISION OF STATE CHILD ABUSE CRIME RECORDS THROUGH THE NATIONAL CRIMINAL HISTORY BACKGROUND CHECK SYSTEM.

1. Not later than 180 days after the date of enactment of this Act, the Attorney General shall, subject to availability of appropriations

    a. investigate the criminal history records system of each State and determine for each State a timetable by which the State should be able to provide child abuse crime records on an online basis through the national criminal history background check system;

    b. in consultation with State officials, establish guidelines for the reporting or indexing of child abuse crime information, including guidelines relating to the format, content, and accuracy of criminal history records and other procedures for carrying out this Act; and

    c. notify each State of the determinations made pursuant to subparagraphs A and B.

2. The Attorney General shall require as a part of each State timetable that the State
    a. by not later than the date that is 3 years after the date of enactment of this Act, have in a computerized criminal history file at least 80 percent of the final dispositions that have been rendered in all identifiable child abuse crime cases in which there has been an event of activity within the last 5 years;
    b. continue to maintain a reporting rate of at least 80 percent for final dispositions in all identifiable child abuse crime cases in which there has been an event of activity within the preceding 5 years; and
    c. take steps to achieve 100 percent disposition reporting, including data quality audits and periodic notices to criminal justice agencies identifying records that lack final dispositions and requesting those dispositions.

C. LIAISON. An authorized agency of a State shall maintain close liaison with the National Center on Child Abuse and Neglect, the National Center for Missing and Exploited Children, and the National Center for the Prosecution of Child Abuse for the exchange of technical assistance in cases of child abuse.

D. ANNUAL SUMMARY.
    1. The Attorney General shall publish an annual statistical summary of child abuse crimes.
    2. The annual statistical summary described in paragraph 1 shall not contain any information that may reveal the identity of any particular victim or alleged violator.

E. ANNUAL REPORT. The Attorney General shall, subject to the availability of appropriations, publish an annual summary of each State's progress in reporting child abuse crime information to the national criminal history background check system.

F. STUDY OF CHILD ABUSE OFFENDERS.
    1. Not later than 180 days after the date of enactment of this Act, the Administrator of the Office of Juvenile Justice and Delinquency Prevention shall begin a study based on a statistically significant sample of convicted child abuse offenders and other relevant information to determine
        a. the percentage of convicted child abuse offenders who have more than 1 conviction for an offense involving child abuse;
        b. the percentage of convicted child abuse offenders who have been convicted of an offense involving child abuse in more than 1 State; and

     c. the extent to which and the manner in which instances of child abuse form a basis for convictions for crimes other than child abuse crimes.

  2. Not later than 1 year after the date of enactment of this Act, the Administrator shall submit a report to the Chairman of the Committee on the Judiciary of the Senate and the Chairman of the Committee on the Judiciary of the House of Representatives containing a description of and a summary of the results of the study conducted pursuant to paragraph 1.

SECTION 3: BACKGROUND CHECKS.

A. IN GENERAL.

  1. A State may have in effect procedures (established by State statute or regulation) that require qualified entities designated by the State to contact an authorized agency of the State to request a nationwide background check for the purpose of determining whether a provider has been convicted of a crime that bears upon an individual's fitness to have responsibility for the safety and wellbeing of children.

  2. The authorized agency shall access and review State and Federal criminal history records through the national criminal history background check system and shall make reasonable efforts to respond to the inquiry within 15 business days.

B. GUIDELINES. The procedures established under subsection (a) shall require

  1. that no qualified entity may request a background check of a provider under subsection (A) unless the provider first provides a set of fingerprints and completes and signs a statement that

     a. contains the name, address, and date of birth appearing on a valid identification document (as defined in section 1028 of title 18, United States Code) of the provider;

     b. the provider has not been convicted of a crime and, if the provider has been convicted of a crime, contains a description of the crime and the particulars of the conviction;

     c. notifies the provider that the entity may request a background check under subsection (A);

     d. notifies the provider of the provider's rights under paragraph 2; and

     e. notifies the provider that prior to the completion of the background check the qualified entity may choose to deny the provider unsupervised access to a child to whom the qualified entity provides child care.

  2. that each provider who is the subject of a background check is entitled

a. to obtain a copy of any background check report; and

b. to challenge the accuracy and completeness of any information contained in any such report and obtain a prompt determination as to the validity of such challenge before a final determination is made by the authorized agency;

3. that an authorized agency, upon receipt of a background check report lacking disposition data, shall conduct research in whatever State and local recordkeeping systems are available in order to obtain complete data;

4. that the authorized agency shall make a determination whether the provider has been convicted of, or is under pending indictment for, a crime that bears upon an individual's fitness to have responsibility for the safety and wellbeing of children and shall convey that determination to the qualified entity; and

5. that any background check under subsection (A) and the results thereof shall be handled in accordance with the requirements of Public Law 92-544.

C. REGULATIONS.

1. The Attorney General may by regulation prescribe such other measures as may be required to carry out the purposes of this Act, including measures relating to the security, confidentiality, accuracy, use, misuse, and dissemination of information, and audits and recordkeeping.

2. The Attorney General shall, to the maximum extent possible, encourage the use of the best technology available in conducting background checks.

D. LIABILITY. A qualified entity shall not be liable in an action for damages solely for failure to conduct a criminal background check on a provider, nor shall a State or political subdivision thereof nor any agency, officer or employee thereof, be liable in an action for damages for the failure of a qualified entity to take action adverse to a provider who was the subject of a background check.

E. FEES. In the case of a background check pursuant to a State requirement adopted after the date of the enactment of this Act conducted with fingerprints on a person who volunteers with a qualified entity, the fees collected by authorized State agencies and the Federal Bureau of Investigation may not exceed the actual cost of the background check conducted with fingerprints. The States shall establish fee systems that ensure that fees to nonprofit entities for background checks do not discourage volunteers from participating in child care programs.

SECTION 4: FINDING FOR IMPROVEMENT OF CHILD ABUSE CRIME INFORMATION.

A. USE OF FORMULA GRANTS FOR IMPROVEMENTS IN STATE RECORDS AND SYSTEMS. Section 509(b) of the Omnibus Crime Control and Safe Streets Act of 1968 (42 U.S.C. 3759(b)) is amended

1. in paragraph 2 by striking 'and' after the semicolon;
2. in paragraph 3 by striking the period and inserting '; and'; and
3. by adding at the end the following new paragraph:
4. 'the improvement of State record systems and the sharing of all of the records described in paragraphs 1, 2, and 3 and the child abuse crime records required under the National Child Protection Act of 1993 with the Attorney General for the purpose of implementing the National Child Protection Act of 1993,'

B. ADDITIONAL FUNDING GRANTS FOR THE IMPROVEMENT OF CHILD ABUSE CRIME INFORMATION.

1. The Attorney General shall, subject to appropriations and with preference to States that, as of the date of enactment of this Act, have in computerized criminal history files the lowest percentages of charges and dispositions of identifiable child abuse cases, make a grant to each State to be used
   a. for the computerization of criminal history files for the purposes of this Act;
   b. for the improvement of existing computerized criminal history files for the purposes of this Act;
   c. to improve accessibility to the national criminal history background check system for the purposes of this Act; and
   d. to assist the State in the transmittal of criminal records to, or the indexing of criminal history record in, the national criminal history background check system for the purposes of this Act.
2. There are authorized to be appropriated for grants under paragraph 1 a total of $20,000,000 for fiscal years 1994, 1995, 1996, and 1997.

C. WITHHOLDING STATE FUNDS. Effective 1 year after the date of enactment of this Act, the Attorney General may reduce, by up to 10 percent, the allocation to a State for a fiscal year under title I of the Omnibus Crime Control and Safe Streets Act of 1968 that is not in compliance with the requirements of this Act.

SECTION 5: DEFINITIONS.

For the purposes of this Act

1. the term 'authorized agency' means a division or office of a State designated by a State to report, receive, or disseminate information under this Act;

2. the term 'child' means a person who is a child for purposes of the criminal child abuse law of a State;

3. the term 'child abuse crime' means a crime committed under any law of a State that involves the physical or mental injury, sexual abuse or exploitation, negligent treatment, or maltreatment of a child by any person;

4. the term 'child abuse crime information' means the following facts concerning a person who has been arrested for, or has been convicted of, a child abuse crime: full name, race, sex, date of birth, height, weight, fingerprints, a brief description of the child abuse crime or offenses for which the person has been arrested or has been convicted, the disposition of the charge, and any other information that the Attorney General determines may be useful in identifying persons arrested for, or convicted of, a child abuse crime;

5. the term 'child care' means the provision of care, treatment, education, training, instruction, supervision, or recreation to children by persons having unsupervised access to a child;

6. the term 'national criminal history background check system' means the criminal history record system maintained by the Federal Bureau of Investigation based on fingerprint identification or any other method of positive identification;

7. the term 'provider' means
    a. a person who
        i.   is employed by or volunteers with a qualified entity;
        ii. who owns or operates a qualified entity; or
        iii. who has or may have unsupervised access to a child to whom the qualified entity provides child care; and
    b. a person who
        i.   seeks to be employed by or volunteer with a qualified entity;
        ii. seeks to own or operate a qualified entity; or
        iii. seeks to have or may have unsupervised access to a child to whom the qualified entity provides child care;

8. the term 'qualified entity' means a business or organization, whether public, private, for-profit, not-for-profit, or voluntary, that provides child care or child care placement services, including a business or organization that licenses or certifies others to provide child care or child care placement services; and

9. the term 'State' means a State, the District of Columbia, the Commonwealth of Puerto Rico, American Samoa, the Virgin Islands, Guam, and the Trust Territories of the Pacific.

Speaker of the House of Representatives.
Vice President of the United States and President of the Senate.

T Appendix

Sample Volunteer Application Form (Churches)

Applicants for a volunteer position that involves the supervision, care, or instruction of children and youth must complete this form. The church uses this form to help ensure a safe and secure environment for those children and youth who participate in its programs and use its facilities. This form, however, is not an employment application. Persons seeking a position as a paid employee are required to complete an employment application.

A. PERSONAL DATA

Name_____

   last   first   middle

Address _____

City _____ State/Prov._____

Zip/Postal Code_____

Phone: Home _____

Cell _____ Work_____

Do you have a current driver's license? _____ If no, please explain. _____

_____

If you will be transporting children or youth, please list your driver's license number:

_____

(Identity may be confirmed with a state driver's license or other photographic identification.)

B. POSITION APPLYING FOR

Please indicate the type of children or youth's work you prefer. _____

_____

Please indicate the date you will be available. _____

_____

What is the minimum length of commitment you can make?_____

_____

C. HISTORY AND PRIOR CHILDREN/YOUTH'S WORK IN A NONPROFIT SETTING

List the churches you have attended regularly during the past five years.

_____

Please indicate your reason(s) for leaving those churches. _____

_____

Please list all previous church work involving youth. _____

_____

Please list all previous non-church work involving youth. _____

_____

How do you communicate your authority to children and youth? _____

_____

What methods of discipline might you use in your position with children and youth?

_____

_____

What training have you received in the care and nurture of children and youth?

_____

_____

List any gifts, education, or other factors that have prepared you for children and youth work.

_____

_____

Describe how you best like to be supervised. _____

_____

D. BACKGROUND CHECK

Have you ever been convicted of or pled guilty or no contest to charges of child abuse or neglect?
Yes_____   No_____

Have you ever been dismissed or terminated from a volunteer or paid position for charges of child abuse or neglect?
Yes_____   No_____

Have you ever been convicted of or pled guilty or no contest to a misdemeanor or a felony?
Yes_____   No_____   If yes, please explain: _____

_____

Have you ever been dismissed or terminated from a volunteer or paid position for allegations of fiscal mismanagement, harassment, or misconduct? Yes_____   No_____   If yes, please explain: _____

_____

The information contained in this application is correct to the best of my knowledge.

Upon consideration of this application, I release any individual, this church or church official, employer, reference or other organization from any and all liability for damages of whatever kind or nature, which may at any time result to me, my heirs, or family on account of compliance or any attempt to comply with this authorization.

I have carefully read the foregoing release and know the contents thereof, and I sign this release of my own free will. This is a legally binding agreement, which I have read and understood.

I have read the child safety policy of this church, and I agree to follow the policies as written.

Applicant's Signature _____

Date_____

If applicant is a minor under State or Provincial law, a parent/guardian's signature is requested.
Applicant's Parent/Guardian Signature _____

Date_____

U Appendix

Sample Volunteer Application Form (Nonprofit Organizations)

Applicants for a volunteer position that involves the supervision, care, or instruction of children and youth must complete this form. The organization uses this form to provide a safe and secure environment for those children and youth who participate in its programs and use its facilities. This form, however, is not an employment application. Persons seeking a position as a paid employee are required to complete an employment application.

A. PERSONAL DATA

Name_____
　　　last　　　　　　　　　first　　　　　　　　　middle

Address _____

City _____ State/Prov._____

Zip/Postal Code_____

Phone: Home _____

Cell _____ Work_____

Do you have a current driver's license? _____If no, please explain. ____

_____

If you will be transporting children or youth, please list your driver's license number:

_____

(Identity may be confirmed with a state driver's license or other photographic identification.)

B. POSITION APPLYING FOR

Please indicate the type of children or youth's work you prefer. _____

Please indicate the date you will be available. _____

What is the minimum length of commitment you can make?_____

C. HISTORY AND PRIOR CHILDREN/YOUTH'S WORK IN A NONPROFIT SETTING

List the other organizations you have volunteered for during the past five years. _____

_____

Please indicate your reason(s) for leaving those organizations. _____

_____

Please list all previous volunteer work involving youth. _____

_____

Please list all previous paid work experience involving youth. _____

_____

How do you communicate your authority to children and youth? _____

_____

What methods of discipline might you use in your position with children and youth?

_____

_____

What training have you received in the care and supervision of children and youth?

_____

_____

List any skills, training, education, or other factors that have prepared you for children and youth work.

_____

_____

Describe how you best like to be supervised. _____

_____

D. BACKGROUND CHECK

Have you ever been convicted of or pled guilty or no contest to charges of child abuse or neglect?
Yes_____   No_____

Have you ever been dismissed or terminated from a volunteer or paid position for charges of child abuse or neglect?
Yes_____   No_____

Have you ever been convicted of or pled guilty or no contest to a misdemeanor or a felony?
Yes_____   No_____   If yes, please explain:

_____

_____

Have you ever been dismissed or terminated from a volunteer or paid position for allegations of fiscal mismanagement, harassment, or misconduct? Yes_____   No_____   If yes, please explain: _____

_____

The information contained in this application is correct to the best of my knowledge.

Upon consideration of this application, I release any individual, this organization or official of the organization, employer, reference or other organization from any and all liability for damages of whatever kind or nature, which may at any time result to me, my heirs, or family on account of compliance or any attempt to comply with this authorization.

I have carefully read the foregoing release and know the contents thereof, and I sign this release of my own free will. This is a legally binding agreement, which I have read and understood.

I have read the child safety policy and I agree to follow it.

Applicant's Signature _____

Date_____

If applicant is a minor under State or Provincial law, a parent/guardian's signature is requested.
Applicant's Parent/Guardian Signature _____

Date_____

V Appendix

Sample Reference Check Form

(Non-relatives, employers, supervisors, or coworkers may be included as references.)

Name_____
      last   first   middle

Address _____

City _____ State/Prov._____

Zip/Postal Code_____

Phone: Home _____

I authorize the listed reference to give you any information (including opinions) they have regarding my character and fitness for child and youth work. I waive any right I may have to inspect any information provided about me by any person identified in this application.

_____   _____

Applicant Signature   Date

How long have you known this person?_____

In what capacity have you known this person? _____

_____

_____

Describe this person's skills/gifts for working with children. _____

_____

Do you have any concerns about this person's prior work with children or his/her relationship with children? _____

_____

Describe how this person interacts with children. _____

_____

_____

Describe how this person disciplines children. _____

_____

_____

Do you have any knowledge about this person's behavior, attitude, or emotions toward children that might cause a parent to worry about this person caring for his/her children? _____

If yes, please specify. _____

_____

_____   _____

Applicant Signature   Date

W Appendix

Guidelines for Integrating Sexual Offenders

Before integrating a sexual offender into a church or nonprofit organization, the organization should consider these three issues: the category of sexual offender, the risk that the person will re-offend, and the method the offender used to communicate his or her past to the organization. After determining these three issues, the organization can look to some guidelines about how to protect its youth and children.

Categories of Sexual Offenders

Known sexual offenders

The first category is the *known sexual offender*, a person either convicted in a court of law or found guilty by an organization's own judicial process. The convicted sex offender's name and offense are a matter of public record and therefore *known*. An organization can learn of a convicted sexual offender by conducting a criminal record check, using the person's name, date of birth, social security number, or aliases and submitting the information to a law enforcement agency.

On the other hand, an adjudicated offense is not often publicly mentioned nor recorded. In fact, most members or constituents of an organization are unaware when an organization conducts an adjudication hearing and what the outcome is. If the organization has affiliates or is affiliated with a larger organization or denomination, it may disseminate the name and offense to others, but is not required to do so. However, this is gradually changing. More organizations are open to making disclosures of allegations as the result of intense media coverage and demands by parents for assurances that their children are in a safe environment.

An exception to public knowledge of the courtroom conviction is the juvenile sexual offender—a minor convicted of a sexual offense. The conviction record of a minor is usually sealed; after the offender becomes an adult, the record remains sealed except for special circumstances.

In nonprofit organizations and churches, a person may confess or be found guilty of an offense in violation of the organization's standard of conduct but not in violation of the community's criminal code. In these instances, the organization takes disciplinary action and the person becomes known as an adjudicated offender. In other instances, the offense may violate the criminal code, but a statute of limitations prevents prosecution or a civil action. In those cases, the organization may adjudicate the complaint—not as a violation of law— but as a violation of the organization's standard of conduct or contrary to a specific job description. However, public mention and dissemination of this information varies substantially by organization and by community.

A statute of limitation sets the length of time the government or a victim has to bring forward a criminal charge or a civil action. The statutes vary in the United States and across the Canadian provinces. In some communities, the statute bars prosecution or civil action as few as six years from the date the incident occurred. In other communities, a statute may waive any period of limitation for sexual crimes committed against a child. Further, the limitations on criminal prosecution may differ from the limitations on civil actions, which tend to be shorter. Because the laws are ever changing, an organization should consult with an attorney when responding to an alleged incident.

In some states and provinces, the names of those convicted of sexual offenses are on a Sex Offender Registry. A person on this list is a registered sex offender. Minors, in most instances, are noticeably absent from these registries. A person who is adjudicated through an organization rather than the courts is also not named on such registries.

States and provinces with a Sex Offender Registry list sexual offenders who were convicted *after* the registry law passed; offenders convicted prior to the registry law will not appear on the registry. For purposes of screening, then, we warn against using the registry as the *only* source of identifying an applicant as a sexual offender. The registry will identify only recently convicted offenders and will not identify minors or adults convicted as minors whose records were sealed.

Unsubstantiated sexual offenders

The second category is the *unsubstantiated sexual offender*, a person who has not been convicted or adjudicated of a sexual offense, but does not deny that he or she committed a sexual offense. Perhaps there is testimony from the victim about the incident, but prosecution or pursuit of civil action has been barred (see sidebar). The offender is likely an older adult now—and may speak of the offense as a youthful indiscretion, the result of stress or poor judgment, or a consensual event, despite laws that criminalize sexual contact with youth, patients, students, clients, parishioners, and so on.

Organizations struggle with how to integrate the unsubstantiated sexual offender into their organization and programs. If a court of law never convicted a person, is it fair to deny the person an opportunity to serve the community? If the person accepts responsibility for the incident and it happened many years ago without any subsequent reports of offense, does the person deserve a second chance?

Unknown sexual offenders

The third category likely has the largest number of people in it—the *unknown sexual offender*. Many sexual offenses are not reported to authorities, and many people accused of abuse deny it to the authorities. As there is no record of a complaint or a conversation with an alleged offender that results in no further action, an organization will be unaware that certain board members, staff members, volunteers, or applicants could be sexual offenders. If the victim and offender keep the offense a secret, and they do not come forward to disclose it, screening tools will not be sufficient to reveal this category of offender. That's why general policies and strong supervision remain essential components of any child safety policy.

Risk of Re-Offense

In addition to understanding the various categories of offenders, organizations should also consider factors that contribute to re-offense. Is the applicant's risk to re-offend high or relatively low? Somewhere in between?

Organizations should seek assistance from a knowledgeable professional when trying to establish the probability of re-offense. Here are some general factors that you might consider along with the other information you receive on an applicant. While no specific item will determine high risk for re-offense, the risk likely increases with each factor that applies to the applicant.

- The offender was convicted of a sexual offense more than once.
- There's a pattern of victims and offenses over time or in different communities.
- The offender's age at the onset of the offenses, the age of the victim(s).
- The number of alleged victims or offenses before the offender was caught.
- The offender's approach to a potential victim—often referred to as "grooming the victim." The greater the manipulation, the harder it is to break the grooming behavior.
- The offender's use of primary defense mechanisms, such as denial, rationalization, minimization, or projection of blame.
- The offender's participation (or lack thereof) in a community-based treatment program or in a treatment program while incarcerated.
- The presence of compulsive and addictive behavior, such as dependence on or addiction to drugs, alcohol, pornography, gambling, prostitution, and so on.
- The offender acknowledges wrongdoing only by projection of blame onto the victim, the aggressive prosecutor, the church official, the ex-spouse, and so on.
- The offender's expression (or lack thereof) of empathy for the victim and remorse for the harm caused the victim.
- The offender acknowledges the "triggers" that led him or her to victimize others and has learned to substitute other conduct when triggers arise; or, the offender seeks opportunities to be with the target population again, refusing to acknowledge those triggers.

Logically, the greater the risk of re-offense, the greater the liability there is for the organization if the offender is integrated. Ethically, the greater the risk of re-offense, the greater the moral duty of the organization to protect the children and youth, if the organization wants to integrate the offender.

Victims and offenders keep the offense secret for different reasons. Why do you think victims might keep the offense a secret? Why would offenders avoid disclosing an offense? What could an organization do to encourage victims to disclose abuse?

A positive sign that a sexual offender is working out his or her recovery plan is when the offender accepts that he or she cannot seek out the former target population. In recovery, the offender begins to realize that triggers may never go away—so he or she learns to stay away.

What to do?

Jerry befriended Carl through a prison program that offers support services to inmates and their families. Carl was serving a lengthy prison term for sexually abusing his two stepdaughters. After Carl's release from prison, Jerry helped him find an apartment and fixed him up with a few furnishings. Carl started to attend Jerry's church, and within a few months he asked to become a member. Jerry's pastor, informed of Carl's history, said that the church's governing body would decide whether to extend membership to Carl. They did extend membership, but they also insisted on sharing Carl's history with the congregation. Carl agreed to a letter of disclosure, but in exchange he asked to give a testimony of his life during a worship service. During his testimony, Carl gave many examples of mistakes that the devil made him make—and how sorry he was. With tears in his eyes, he invited the congregation to befriend him because he was a changed man. Some people did extend friendship to Carl, and, despite the letter of disclosure, a few parents invited Carl to spend time with their families. Although monitored, Carl continued to evade his supervisors and looked for opportunities to be alone with youth.

Method of Disclosure

The third issue when considering whether to integrate a person who has been a sexual offender is to identify his or her disclosure method. In other words, did the person disclose his or her history or did the organization discover it about him or her? It is important to remember that self-disclosure should not necessarily put the organization at ease.

The sexual offender discloses past sexual conviction or history of abuse.

A sexual offender may approach an organization seeking a job, a volunteer assignment, or membership in the organization. The offender may disclose a past conviction or history of abuse because he or she

- wants to ease concern by revealing the information first;
- is led to the organization by another member or volunteer, and through their relationship, the offender's history is revealed;
- was not held accountable for abusive behavior and does not understand the threat he or she represents;
- projects blame for being caught on another person;
- denies that his or her behavior was wrong or harmful;
- intends to gain access to a target population to re-offend; or
- is attracted to the organization's resolve to restore or rehabilitate the person.

Joining an organization that serves children or youth gives a sexual offender access to potential victims. To alleviate concern, the offender may disclose a prior conviction to persuade the organization that the behavior is in the past. The person wants to convince the organization of his or her honesty, saying, in effect, "I'm telling you this because I'm a changed person." The offender may try to convince the organization that working with youth is part of a personal renewal to correct serious behavioral flaws of the past.

Sexual offense is a betrayal of trust by someone who shows little regard for the harm he or she inflicts or for its long-term consequences for the victim. Therefore, organizations have reason to be suspicious of these disclosures. An organization that approves the application of a sexual offender has virtually no defense against a claim of negligence if that volunteer or staff member re-offends. More importantly, the organization will have violated its fiduciary duty to protect children and youth from a foreseeable risk of harm.

The organization discovers the sexual offender's history.

A sexual offender may approach an organization looking for a job, a volunteer assignment, or membership in the organization. Often the shame of incarceration or the pain of being shunned by family or community can lead an offender to hide his or her past conduct.

However, *denial* of past wrongful behavior usually plays a more significant role in the person's failure to disclose a previous history of abuse. Part of this denial includes rationalizing one's behavior or minimizing its effects on the victim or others. Examples include:

- "She never said she didn't want my *affection*."
- "It's not like I broke someone's arm."
- "Kids *claim* abuse because they know that will get parents or leaders in trouble."

The offender often denies that he or she is still subject to the triggers that led to abusive behavior, and denies as well a need for treatment, supervision, or accountability. Statements such as "I should be forgiven and allowed to move on" suggest denial on the part of the offender that his or her past behavior could warrant continuing consequences.

What results when we put *categories of offenders* + *risk of re-offense* + *disclosure method* together?

Guidelines to Protect Children and Youth from Sexual Offenders in Faith-Based Organizations

Known sexual offenders
If the following scenarios exist, the governing body of the church and the known offender should sign a *Covenant of Conduct.*

- Scenario 1: the known offender asks to join or become a member and has disclosed a previous conviction or adjudication for sexual offense.
- Scenario 2: the offender asks to join or become a member and is discovered to be a convicted or adjudicated sexual offender through interviewing or screening.
- Scenario 3: the offender asks to rejoin (a former member of the church) or join as a transfer from another congregation and has a previous conviction or adjudication for sexual offense.

The *Covenant of Conduct* should include the following items:

- The individual verifies the history of the offense, conviction, or adjudication disclosed to the governing body.
- The individual consents to disclosing the history of the offense, conviction, or adjudication to the congregation, usually via a letter to parents who can decide what precautions they wish to take on behalf of their children

What to do?
Jed had volunteered for KIDS 'R' GR8 for several years. Popular with teen boys, Jed was a former college standout in basketball and always had a pick-up game going on at KIDS or in his driveway at home. Marlys was the volunteer coordinator for KIDS. She started calling Jed in November to verify that he would return in January for another year of volunteering. Jed's wife apologized but kept repeating that Jed was out of town and unavailable. She promised to give him the message—but Jed did not return Marlys's call. When she hadn't been able to reach Jed by Christmas time, she asked other volunteers if they had heard from him. One volunteer said he hadn't and commented that it was like Jed just dropped off the face of the earth. Marlys wasn't too alarmed, but she did wonder how she'd explain Jed's absence to the teens.

To run the last few volunteer criminal record checks, she booted up the computer and on a whim, she searched the state's sex offender registry. She typed in the zip code where Jed lived. There, on the screen—Jed had been convicted of soliciting a minor for immoral purposes in September and was sentenced to prison.

When a nonprofit organization encounters an applicant who hides the past, the organization cannot trust this person in the future. Organizations increase their risk of liability when approving an offender as a staff person or volunteer in a youth program even with safeguards and policies in place. Organizations should not neglect their duty to protect the children and youth in their care.

- The individual covenants that he or she will not participate in any children or youth ministry activities apart from the worship service, including no visits to classrooms or activity centers.
- The individual covenants that he or she will not participate in any volunteer activity with children or youth, supervision or leadership role or activity, or off-site youth program-sponsored activities, such as mission events, community projects with youth, and so on.
- The individual consents to supervision throughout the time he or she attends activities in the worship center, including use of the restroom
- The individual covenants to refrain from engaging youth in private conversations away from the worship center, in places such as the parking lot, narthex, fellowship room, stairwells, classrooms, restroom, and so on.

The *Covenant of Conduct* should also address the following items:
- Any restrictions imposed on the offender are subject to review. (The organization should impose restrictions for a minimum of three years with periodic reviews.) If the offender is absent from the organization for a period of six to eight weeks or longer, the restriction is lengthened for the time absent.
- The governing body determines other activities the sexual offender may be barred from (for example, performing in a drama or choir, serving as liturgist, and so on).
- The faith-based organization should cooperate with any court order, probation order, restraining order, or treatment regimen that affects the sexual offender's contact with minors or other vulnerable persons.
- The church will report any suspected sexual offense to civil authorities immediately.
- Any violation of the *Covenant of Conduct*, including any allegation or suspicion of abusive behavior, will result in steps of discipline, including a ban from the facility.

If a known offender applies for a volunteer or staff position, the church should deny the offender an opportunity with any activity, program, or position that involves youth or puts the offender in a position of trust and authority. The church's governing body should consult legal counsel whenever a known sexual offender applies for a volunteer or staff position, as the governing body may be liable for screening failures, supervision failures, and reporting failures.

If a sexual offender does not disclose a conviction or adjudication, and the church learns of it later, the offender should be removed from any paid or volunteer position. The person must also agree to sign a Covenant of Conduct and face steps of discipline.

What to do about an unsubstantiated sexual offender in a church?
This question leads to great debate among church leaders and church members. Often, someone will admit to an abuse or misconduct in the past, and there will be no report of any subsequent wrongdoing. Is the person covering up other incidents? Or did he or she engage in a serious offense just once? If it's the former, then that person may pose an ongoing risk. However, if it's the latter, that person may pose minimal risk. And, if the risk is indeed minimal, and the person has admitted wrongdoing, shouldn't we offer the person another opportunity to serve?

Actually, the issue at stake here is *consequences*. The offender, already seemingly forgiven for something that harmed another, may still face a family, an organization, or an entire community that decides a consequence should remain in place for an extended time. Distrust and betrayal have upset an established equilibrium in the family or community, and the offense or abuse has led to confusion and anger. A family, church, or community may conclude that victims of abuse struggle with issues of trust and betrayal for many years—and justice requires offenders to live with the consequences of their actions for many years, too.

The faith community should demonstrate to victims that it understands the profound impact and long-term effects of abuse. There's much to learn about justice-making, restoration, and reconciliation between the offender and the victim and between the offender and the church community. Models of justice and reconciliation are still being developed. In the meantime, the church community needs to remember its responsibility to protect children and youth from harm. When former offenders who pose even a small risk are denied an opportunity to work with youth, it reflects a decision to err on the side of caution for the sake of children.

We suggest that the church deny the application of an unsubstantiated sexual offender when:
- the offense occurred within ten years of the volunteer or employment application; and
- the offender did not disclose the complaint or admission during the application process; and
- the position in question is working with youth or serving in a position of trust and authority.

After the ten-year point, the church may consider the volunteer or staff applicant for a position when:

- the applicant has been held accountable by the victim for the harm caused (this means the offender identifies the victim and the victim is interviewed about the accountability); and
- the position is not one of trust or authority or a position in which he or she will be alone with youth.

Guidelines to Protect Children and Youth from Sexual Offenders in Nonprofit Organization

Known sexual offenders in a nonprofit organization
A convicted or adjudicated sexual offender might apply to join or to volunteer or work for an organization in order to have contact with the population served by that organization (usually children or youth). In light of the fiduciary duty and liability, the organization should *not* approve this person. Under the organization's child safety policy, it should deny the applicant the opportunity. The organization should consult with legal counsel if they are concerned about denying any applicant.

Similarly, if the organization learns that a current volunteer, staff, or board member is a convicted or adjudicated sexual offender, the organization should consult legal counsel, and under the child safety policy, the organization should remove the person from his or her duties.

Unsubstantiated sexual offenders in a nonprofit organization
Because information about the unsubstantiated sexual offender is not easy to obtain, an organization must use the tools and policies at its disposal to protect the children and youth in its care. In doing so, if there's a reasonable belief that the individual engaged in misconduct or abuse, the organization should reserve the right to deny the applicant a position. And again, the organization should consult legal counsel.

If the unsubstantiated sexual offender does not deny allegations of abuse or misconduct that happened within the last ten years, the organization should deny the person a paid or volunteer position.

If the unsubstantiated sexual offender does not deny allegations of abuse that occurred over ten years ago, the organization should not offer the person a position unless

- the governing body is fully aware of the allegations and the applicant's response to them; and

- the governing body consults with the organization's legal counsel before approval of the applicant; and
- the board ensures that the fiduciary duty to the children, their parents, and their organization supersedes the applicant's desire to serve that organization; and
- the applicant is restricted to activities or programs that *always* include another adult co-leader who is aware of the applicant's history; and
- the position does not involve youth or a position of trust and authority.

When a multi-service, nonprofit organization offers programs for adults and minors, the cautions might be harder to enforce because the sexual offender may claim he or she is seeking to participate in the adult programs. Assessing the intent of either the convicted or the unsubstantiated sexual offender could be very difficult; however, the multi-service organization should take available precautions and policies to deny the person opportunity to volunteer or serve in the programs for children or youth.

People who betray the trust of children or youth—and the organization that placed them in a position of trust—often do not accept responsibility for their actions or acknowledge the long-term consequences of their actions on the victim and the organization. Sexual offenders characteristically lack empathy, failing to understand the full extent of the harm they've caused. That's why they rationalize and minimize their actions. They use words like *consent, indiscretion,* and *bad judgment* rather than *assault, violation, crime, repentance, accountability,* and so on.

Sexual offenders who do not disclose past offenses
Whether the church or nonprofit organization serves primarily youth or is a multi-service organization, the organization should thoroughly screen applicants and implement adequate supervision safeguards. If the organization becomes aware through the screening process that an applicant is a convicted or adjudicated sexual offender, the organization should deny that person an opportunity to serve with children or youth or to serve in a position of trust and authority.

Unknown sexual offenders
If information obtained through references and interviews creates a reasonable suspicion that a person has committed a sexual offense, the organization may deny the applicant a position; or the organization could seek additional information about the applicant to corroborate or put to rest the suspicion.

The organization should have a policy that states *it reserves the right to reject any applicant for any reason.* The organization may implement this decision at the time a reasonable suspicion arises. The organization should store and keep confidential any written material or record of a conversation or reference disclosing information leading to a reasonable suspicion.

Sexual offenders who are minors
As stated earlier, a minor convicted of a sexual offense receives some protection by the juvenile courts. Authorities will not disclose a minor's criminal record, and organizations cannot access information about a minor's conviction. Because a minor's record usually remains closed even after he or she becomes an adult, organizations are caught in the middle. They cannot learn the information that would help them protect the children entrusted to their care.

So the minor who offended creates a screening challenge for organizations. Therefore, as a best practice policy, older minors should not spend time alone with younger minors during youth programs, nor should they supervise or care for children or youth without adult supervision. They should not be placed in situations where they spend time alone with program participants, such as off-site activities, in a vehicle, in a home, or another private setting.

When an organization does learn of a minor who is a sexual offender, it should bar that minor from volunteering in programs for children and youth. In addition, the organization should prohibit the offender from access to younger minors in the organization's facility. The organization should obey all known court-imposed orders and treatment requirements. Volunteers or staff must supervise the minor's contacts on-site, in parking lots, when participating in organization-sponsored transportation, and during all off-site activities sponsored by the organization.

Organizations may bar the offender's participation in age-appropriate programs, too. If the offender is allowed to participate, but then violates policies or established rules or engages in inappropriate behavior, the organization should remove the minor immediately. Depending on the behavior, the organization may report the individual to civil authorities. The organization may reinstate the minor to the program only when his or her risk of inappropriate behavior is reduced.

If the organization becomes aware of an offender who is a minor and yet cannot disclose the information, the organization should remove the offender if he or she is in a volunteer position or deny the minor any opportunity to volunteer.

Further, an organization should minimize the risk of an unknown juvenile offender by requiring all applicants who are minors to submit to the allowable screening steps. The organization should document the steps that it has taken to reasonably reduce the risk the applicant might pose to children or youth. With adequate supervision and accountability policies, the organization is able to take reasonable precautions while acknowledging that some risk remains.

 Appendix

Recommended Screening Steps for Church Positions

	Application	Interview	References	Criminal Check	Finger-printing
Pastor	X	X	X	X	X
Ordained staff	X	X	X	X	X
Non-ordained staff	X	X	X	X	X
Professional staff	X	X	X	X	X
Counseling staff	X	X	X	X	X
Choir/Music director	X	X	X	X	X
Youth program director	X	X	X	X	X
Youth program supervisor	X	X	X	X	X
Staff/Volunteer supervisor	X	X	X	X	X
Youth group leader	X	X	X	X	X
Head leader of Girl's Club	X	X	X	X	
Head leader of Boy's Club	X	X	X	X	
Superintendent	X	X	X		
Head nursery attendant	X	X	X		
Janitor	X	X	X	X	
Secretary	X	X	X		
Bookkeeper	X	X	X	X	
Bus driver	X	X	X	X	
Girl's Club leader	X	X	X		
Boys Club leader	X	X	X		
Other leaders	X	X	X		
Church school teachers	X	X			
Children's worship teachers	X	X			
Parents as classroom volunteers	X				
Hall monitors	X				
Minors as helpers/aides	X				
Nursery attendants	X				

Y Appendix

Recommended Screening Steps for Positions in a Nonprofit Organization

	Application	Interview	References	Criminal Check	Finger-printing
Executive Director	X	X	X	X	X
Associate Director	X	X	X	X	X
Staff supervisor	X	X	X	X	X
Professional staff	X	X	X	X	X
Counseling staff	X	X	X	X	X
Program director	X	X	X	X	X
Board member	X	X	X	X	
Volunteer supervisor	X	X	X	X	
Youth leader	X	X	X	X	
Mentor	X	X	X	X	
Coach	X	X	X	X	
Building manager	X	X	X		
Recreational leader	X	X	X		
Janitor	X	X	X	X	
Administrative assistant	X	X	X		
Accountant/bookkeeper	X	X	X	X	
Van/bus driver	X	X	X	X	
Grant writer	X	X			
Chaperone	X	X			
Parent-classroom volunteer	X				
Hall monitor	X				
Minors as helpers	X				
Kitchen staff	X				

Z Appendix

Responding to Families Notified of Alleged Abuse

Here are some guidelines for situations in which you have responsibility for talking with families about an alleged abuse against one of their children.

- Remain calm and nonjudgmental.
- Anyone who makes a report to the police or child protection authorities is usually granted anonymity so do not identify the reporter unless you are given permission to do so.
- Do not share any statements made by the child with a parent or relative implicated by the child as an abuser. It is advisable not to share the child's statements with anyone other than the authorities until the identity of the abuser can be determined and authorities have determined whether the child is protected from contact with that person.
- Do not attempt to convince a parent that the alleged abuse happened or did not happen; do not attempt to discredit the child or cast suspicion on the alleged abuser.
- Do not investigate with a parent or family member what may be happening in the home, and do not share information with a parent that has not been shared with the authorities.
- Do not make promises to a parent or family member about the outcome of the investigation.
- Listen to any information a parent may offer about the incident and record it immediately after the conversation; report additional information to authorities through the reporting procedure outlined in the church or nonprofit organization's policy.
- Offer the parent(s) emotional support; this may be necessary for several months.
- Suggest resources for the parent(s) including books or literature that may be helpful to them. Later, counseling resources may be necessary for the parent(s), child, or the family.
- Allow the parent(s) to express disbelief, anger, and grief; the parent(s) may be in shock or denial at the mention of abuse allegations.

- Do not minimize the type of abuse, its impact on the child, or its harm to the child.
- Assure the parent(s) of the need to maintain privacy unless disclosure is necessary to protect the well-being of other children.

AA Appendix

Help Protect Your Children from Abuse

It is not easy for parents to talk to their children about abuse. Parents do not always know what or how much to tell their children. The more children know about abuse and abusers the better they will be able to protect themselves and the more likely they will be to tell their parents what is happening to them.

Ideas to help your children

- Start out talking about other survival information such as how to cross the street safely, petting strange animals, and so on, and include information on abuse issues.
- Find out what your children already know. Teach your children the names for their body parts—teach them that there are parts of their bodies that are private and that no one has the right to touch them without their permission. Clear up any misconceptions.
- Help your children practice saying no to a touch that makes them feel uncomfortable or that they don't understand.
- Encourage family activities like "what if" games that help your children think about new kinds of situations that could occur—activities that can help your children feel surer of their abilities to handle new situations, to trust their instincts, and to act in their own best interest.

What to Tell Your Children

- "Your body is your own—you don't have to let anyone touch you or hurt you."
- "You have my permission to say no or 'don't touch me in that way' to anyone—even a close relative or family friend."
- "If you get uncomfortable feelings when someone does something to you or asks you to do something to them, **come and tell me**."
- "Sometimes nice people—people you know—do mean things. Respecting and 'minding' adults does not mean you have to do anything they ask. If you think what they are doing or asking is wrong, **come and tell me**."

- "If anyone, even someone you love, threatens you or tries to bribe you into doing something you feel is not right, **come and tell me.**"
- "Girls don't always have to please adults, and boys don't always have to be brave and not run away."
- "Some secrets—like surprise birthday presents—are fun, but a secret that an adult says only the two of you can know is not right; **come and tell me.**"
- "If any person touches you in a way that makes you feel uncomfortable, **come and tell me**; I will believe you and protect you. It's not your fault."

Responding to the Abused Child

An important factor in a child's ability to recover is the reaction of the person the child tells about the abuse. As responsible adults, what do we say and do? The following suggestions may help you and your child cope with a disclosure.

- *Believe what they are telling you.* Children rarely lie about abuse
- *Listen.* Go to a private place away from the distractions of other children, TV, and so on. Let them tell their story in their own words. If the child has difficulty verbalizing, drawing pictures or using dolls might help.
- *Do not ask "why" questions* because they tend to lay blame on the child (for example, "Why didn't you run away?"). Make sure the child knows that it is not his or her fault.
- *Remain calm.* The child will believe that your anger, shock, or horror is directed at him or her.
- *Reassure the child* that he or she did the right thing by telling, that the child is not to blame, that you are sorry this has happened, that this has happened to many other children, that these children had the same feelings, and that they recovered and so will your child. Reassure the child that you will do your best to get the help he or she needs and to protect the child from further abuse.
- *Keep your opinions of the offender to yourself,* while placing full responsibility on his or her shoulders. Many children are victims of someone they have loved and trusted, and your negative comments may be perceived by the child to be a reflection of his or her worth as well.
- *Do not confront the offender.* This could impair a formal investigation by giving the offender time to invent a story. Also, a perpetrator can plant seeds of doubt in your mind about the truth of your child's story.
- *Report the abuse* to the police and to a child protection agency. Most children want the offender to get help and want to protect other

children from abuse. *Abusers will not seek help voluntarily and will not stop offending on their own.*

- *Get counseling for your child.* The emotional aftermath of sexual abuse will not disappear by itself. Your child will need to resolve many issues that can be dealt with more effectively with the help of professionals.
- *Support your child.* Respect her or his privacy, keep a routine, and answer questions calmly.